how to start a fitness coaching and training business

A Step-by-Step Guide to Profitable Fitness Programs and Personal Trainer Entrepreneurship

harper wells

contents

introduction

· · ·

IN THE WORLD OF FITNESS, the leap from passion to profession is a journey filled with potential, challenges, and transformative rewards. "How to Start a Fitness Coaching and Training Business: A Step-by-Step Guide to Profitable Fitness Programs and Personal Trainer Entrepreneurship" is your roadmap to navigating this exciting terrain. This book isn't just a collection of strategies and tips; it's a beacon guiding you through the multifaceted landscape of the fitness industry.

LET'S embark on this exploration together, starting with understanding the fitness industry landscape. The realm of fitness coaching is as varied as it is vibrant, encompassing everything from high-intensity interval training to mindful yoga practices. Recognizing your niche within this diverse spectrum is the cornerstone of building a successful coaching business. It's about finding that unique space where your passion meets market demand, a place where you can thrive by doing what you love.

AS WE DELVE DEEPER, assessing the market becomes our first significant step. Here, we'll dive into the current and emerging trends in fitness, gaining insights into what drives the industry forward. Understanding these trends isn't just about keeping up; it's about leveraging them to carve out a unique position for your business. We'll also get to know our potential clients - their needs, preferences, and spending habits - tailoring our fitness services to meet them where they are.

NEXT, we enter the realm of establishing your brand. Here, we talk about creating a unique brand identity, one that resonates with your target audience and sets you apart in the crowded fitness market. This section is about more than logos and color schemes; it's about developing a fitness philosophy that reflects your coaching style and attracts the clientele you wish to serve.

BUT WHAT'S a brand without visibility? Building an online presence and implementing SEO strategies for enhanced visibility is your bridge to reaching a broader audience. Alongside this, we'll explore the power of networking and partnerships, leveraging these connections for business growth and community building.

AS YOU EDGE CLOSER to launching your venture, understanding legal and financial considerations becomes paramount. From navigating legalities to setting up robust financial systems, this part of your journey is about laying a strong foundation for your business. Insurance, liability, pricing strategies - we cover it all, ensuring you're equipped to build a business that's not just fit but also financially healthy.

DESIGNING profitable fitness programs is where your expertise as a coach shines. Balancing client needs with business objectives is an art, and this section is your canvas. We'll explore various training modalities, innovative program design, and marketing strategies to help you craft programs that aren't just effective but also lucrative.

· · ·

As YOU BUILD your client base, the focus shifts to attracting and retaining a robust clientele. Here, we delve into strategies for identifying your ideal client, effective advertising techniques, leveraging social proof, and creating a community around your brand. Client retention is as crucial as acquisition, and we'll guide you through providing exceptional service, engaging communication, and program adaptation to keep your clients coming back.

LASTLY, mastering the art of personal trainer entrepreneurship is about wearing multiple hats. You're not just a coach; you're a businessperson, a marketer, a communicator. Developing an entrepreneurial mindset, acquiring essential business skills, managing finances, and continuously learning and developing - these are the pillars of a successful fitness entrepreneur.

THIS BOOK IS NOT JUST about imparting knowledge; it's about sparking inspiration and empowering you to take action. Each chapter is packed with practical advice, real-world examples, and actionable steps to guide you on your path to building a thriving fitness coaching business. So, let's turn the page and begin this exciting journey together, transforming your passion for fitness into a successful entrepreneurial venture.

laying the foundation for your fitness coaching business

. . .

IN THE VIBRANT world of fitness, finding your spot is like picking the perfect apple in a vast orchard. Every apple has its unique flavor, and in fitness, each coach brings their distinct style and expertise. Our journey begins with a clear understanding of the fitness industry landscape, setting the stage for you to discover and polish your niche in fitness coaching.

IMAGINE WALKING into a gym filled with different equipment. Each machine, from treadmills to weights, has a specific purpose, much like the various niches in fitness coaching. Some trainers excel in high-intensity interval training, while others find their calling in yoga or strength training. In this ever-evolving field, the key is to identify not just what you're good at, but what ignites your passion. That's where your unique coaching style will shine brightest.

UNDERSTANDING the fitness landscape means looking at the big picture. It's about seeing how trends like wearable tech or home workouts fit into people's lives. It's about recognizing the diversity in client needs – some seek weight loss, others want to build muscle, and many are in search of a healthier lifestyle. Your role as a coach isn't just about crafting workout plans; it's about being a guide, a motivator, and sometimes, a life changer.

BUT HOW DO you stand out in a crowded room? This is where identifying your niche becomes crucial. Think of it as planting your flag on a hill that's uniquely yours. Your niche could be anything from training busy professionals who have only 30 minutes a day to spare, to specializing in postnatal fitness. It's about finding that intersection where your skills, passion, and client needs meet.

AS WE DELVE DEEPER, we'll explore the various facets of the fitness industry, from the latest trends and client demographics to understanding your competitors. This isn't just about data; it's about weaving that data into a strategy that sets your fitness coaching business apart. It's about building a foundation on which your unique brand of coaching will thrive.

EACH STEP forward will bring you closer to defining your distinct place in the fitness world. It's not just about being another fitness coach; it's about being the coach that clients seek for that special something only you can offer. As you read on, imagine yourself crafting a fitness philosophy that resonates with your ideal client, one that speaks directly to their goals and challenges. This isn't just the start of a chapter; it's the beginning of a transformation – for both you and your future clients.

Part 1: Assessing the Market

Analyzing Fitness Industry Trends

IN THE DYNAMIC landscape of fitness, staying ahead means understanding the winds of change. Picture a small, bustling gym in a vibrant city. Its success wasn't an accident but a result of its owner, Mia, who had a knack for spotting fitness trends before they became mainstream. Mia's gym, once a traditional weightlifting haven, transformed into a hub for holistic wellness, offering everything from high-intensity interval training to mindfulness yoga. This change wasn't just intuitive; it was backed by meticulous analysis of emerging fitness trends. Mia's story is a testament to the power of understanding and leveraging these trends to carve out a unique position in the fitness coaching world.

Now, let's delve into how you can harness this power for your fitness coaching business. The fitness industry, like fashion, is always evolving, driven by changes in consumer preferences, technology, and scientific research. To tap into this ever-changing landscape, it's crucial to keep an eye on both current and emerging trends.

FIRST, consider wearable technology. Fitness trackers and smartwatches have revolutionized how people approach their health. These devices track everything from steps taken to calories burned and sleep patterns. As a fitness coach, integrating wearable tech into your programs could attract a tech-savvy clientele. Imagine designing workouts that sync with these devices, providing clients with real-time feedback and personalized recommendations based on their data.

· · ·

ANOTHER SIGNIFICANT TREND is the rise of home workouts. The recent global events have accelerated this trend, with more people looking for effective ways to exercise within the confines of their homes. This shift presents an opportunity for you to offer online coaching, virtual classes, and home workout plans. Think about how you can create engaging and challenging routines that require minimal equipment but deliver maximum results.

THEN THERE'S the growing awareness of holistic health. People are no longer content with just physical fitness; they want mental and emotional well-being too. This holistic approach includes practices like yoga, meditation, and stress management. By incorporating these elements into your coaching, you can cater to a broader audience seeking a more rounded approach to health.

NUTRITION IS ALSO a key player in the fitness world. With a surge in interest in diets like keto, vegan, and intermittent fasting, nutritional advice has become an integral part of fitness coaching. Whether you're providing meal plans or collaborating with nutritionists, integrating dietary advice can add immense value to your services.

GROUP FITNESS CLASSES have evolved as well. They're no longer just about aerobics or spinning. Now, there's a variety of options like dance cardio, boot camps, and circuit training. These classes offer not just a workout but also a sense of community. Developing unique group fitness programs can help you attract a diverse group of clients who enjoy the social aspect of exercising.

ANOTHER TREND that's gaining traction is personalized fitness. With the abundance of generic workout plans available, people are looking for programs tailored to their specific needs and goals. This individualization can range from custom workout routines to personalized coaching sessions. By offering bespoke services, you can differentiate yourself in a market saturated with one-size-fits-all solutions.

NEXT, let's look at the rise of recovery-focused fitness. It's not just about pushing hard; it's about recovering smart. This trend includes practices like foam rolling, stretching, and using recovery tools like massage guns. Incorporating these into your coaching can help clients see better results and reduce the risk of injury.

OUTDOOR FITNESS IS ALSO MAKING a comeback. With people craving fresh air and natural settings, outdoor workouts like boot camps, yoga in the park, and hiking groups are becoming popular. These sessions offer a break from the gym's four walls and connect people with nature, which can be a refreshing change for many.

LASTLY, the importance of mental health in fitness is increasingly recognized. This trend sees a focus on exercises that not only strengthen the body but also the mind. As a coach, acknowledging and incorporating mental health practices into your fitness routines can make your offerings more comprehensive and appealing.

Now, how do you leverage these trends to find your unique position? It starts with research. Stay updated with industry reports, attend fitness expos, and engage with your fitness community. Then, reflect on your strengths and interests. What aspects of fitness are you most passionate about? How can you blend these interests with current trends to create something unique?

FOR INSTANCE, if you're passionate about technology and fitness, you could specialize in tech-driven fitness coaching. Or, if you have a background in dance, consider developing dance-based fitness classes that tap into the trend of fun, high-energy workouts.

THE KEY IS to not just follow trends blindly but to adapt them in a way that aligns with your personal brand and what you stand for as a fitness coach. Remember, trends come and go, but what will set you apart is how you interpret these trends to create something that resonates with your target audience.

IN CONCLUSION, analyzing and leveraging fitness industry trends is not just about staying relevant; it's about being a step ahead in a competitive market. It's about creating a unique niche that sets you apart and appeals to your ideal client. By doing so, you're not just following the wave – you're helping to shape the future of fitness.

Understanding Client Demographics

WHO ARE the people walking through your gym's doors, and what do they seek in their fitness journey? Understanding client demographics is like piecing together a puzzle where each piece represents a unique set of needs, preferences, and spending habits. In a world where fitness trends are as diverse as the people embracing them, tailoring your services to meet these varying client demographics becomes a cornerstone for success in the fitness coaching business.

DEMOGRAPHICS IN FITNESS coaching encompass a wide range – from busy professionals looking for quick, high-intensity workouts to seniors seeking gentle, mobility-enhancing exercises. Each demographic group presents distinct needs and preferences. For instance, a recent survey by the International Health, Racquet & Sportsclub Association (IHRSA) highlighted a growing demand among millennials for boutique fitness experiences that offer community and specialization, while baby boomers tend to prioritize low-impact workouts that promote longevity and health preservation.

To TAILOR your fitness services effectively, start by profiling potential clients. This involves understanding not just their age or occupation but delving deeper into their lifestyle, fitness goals, and even their daily schedules. Imagine a young mother who can only spare 30 minutes in a day versus a retired individual with ample free time. Their fitness needs, availability, and even motivation will differ significantly.

ANOTHER CRUCIAL ASPECT IS UNDERSTANDING CLIENTS' spending habits. The Global Wellness Institute reports an increasing willingness among consumers to invest in health and wellness, including fitness services. However, spending capacity can vary widely. Some clients may be willing to invest heavily in personalized training, while others might prefer budget-friendly group classes. Offering a range of services with varied price points can help cater to this diverse financial spectrum.

ONE EFFECTIVE STRATEGY is to conduct regular surveys or informal discussions to gather feedback and insights directly from your clients. This direct communication can reveal what clients value most in their fitness routines – be it flexibility, variety, personal attention, or technological integration. For instance, a client feedback survey might uncover a high demand for yoga and mindfulness sessions among your clientele, steering you to incorporate these into your service offerings.

MOREOVER, staying updated with local and global fitness trends is pivotal. For example, the American College of Sports Medicine's annual survey can provide valuable insights into trending workouts and fitness technologies. Integrating such trends into your offerings can keep your services fresh and appealing.

IT'S ALSO about creating a community that resonates with your client base. Whether it's through social media groups, fitness challenges, or community events, fostering a sense of belonging can be a powerful tool in attracting and retaining clients. Remember, for many, fitness is not just a physical activity; it's a social one.

PERSONALIZATION PLAYS A KEY ROLE HERE. In an era where customization is king, clients appreciate services that cater to their unique needs. This could mean offering personalized workout and nutrition plans, flexible scheduling, or even virtual coaching options for those who can't make it to the gym. Technology can be a great enabler here, with fitness apps and online platforms providing avenues for tailored fitness experiences.

IN TAILORING YOUR SERVICES, don't forget the power of branding. Your brand should speak to the demographic you aim to attract. For instance, if you're targeting young professionals, your branding could be energetic, modern, and emphasize efficiency and results. Conversely, a focus on seniors might mean a brand that communicates care, accessibility, and community.

UNDERSTANDING AND CATERING to client demographics is not just about offering a range of services. It's about creating experiences that resonate with different groups, understanding their unique fitness journeys, and aligning your offerings with their evolving needs. By doing so, you position yourself not just as a fitness coach but as a vital partner in your clients' path to wellness. As you move forward in this chapter, keep in mind that the key to success lies in empathy, adaptability, and a deep understanding of the diverse tapestry of clients you serve.

Competitor Analysis

"KNOW your enemy and know yourself; in a hundred battles, you will never be defeated." This ancient adage by Sun Tzu in 'The Art of War' resonates profoundly when it comes to understanding the competitive landscape in the fitness industry. The journey to carving a unique niche in fitness coaching is not just about understanding your clients but also about comprehensively researching and understanding your competitors. This knowledge is the keystone in identifying gaps in the market and positioning your fitness services uniquely.

THE FIRST STEP in competitor analysis is conducting thorough research. This involves more than just a cursory glance at other fitness businesses in your area. Dive deep into their service offerings, marketing strategies, client reviews, and even their pricing models. Tools like SWOT analysis (Strengths, Weaknesses, Opportunities, Threats) can be invaluable in systematically breaking down what your competitors are doing right and where they might be lacking.

FOR INSTANCE, a detailed analysis might reveal that while many fitness centers in your area offer weight loss programs, few provide holistic wellness plans that integrate mental health practices. Such insights are goldmines for identifying gaps in the market.

ONE EFFECTIVE METHOD is to become a customer of your competitors. Attend their classes, use their services, and note what they do well and where they fall short. This immersive approach can offer insights you might not get from outside observation alone. For instance, you might notice that while a competitor has state-of-the-art equipment, their customer service is lacking. This could be an area where you could excel.

. . .

ANOTHER ASPECT TO consider is technological adoption. Are your competitors leveraging technology to its fullest potential? An analysis might reveal that while many have sophisticated workout equipment, few are utilizing digital platforms for client engagement and retention. This could be an opportunity for you to integrate fitness apps or online coaching into your offerings.

UNDERSTANDING your competitors also involves keeping an eye on emerging trends in the fitness industry and how these are being adopted by others. For instance, if virtual reality (VR) fitness experiences are becoming popular globally, is there a competitor in your local market who has already started offering such experiences? If not, this could be an unexplored opportunity for you.

CLIENT DEMOGRAPHICS PLAY a crucial role in competitor analysis. By understanding the clientele that your competitors cater to, you can identify underserved markets. For example, if most local fitness centers focus on young adults, there might be an opportunity to cater to older adults or teenagers.

FURTHERMORE, ANALYZE YOUR COMPETITORS' marketing and branding strategies. What messages are they conveying? Are they positioning themselves as premium, budget-friendly, or specialty fitness providers? Understanding this can help you find a unique voice and brand positioning that sets you apart.

IT'S ALSO crucial to monitor your competitors over time and not just as a one-time exercise. Markets evolve, and so do the strategies of your competitors. Regularly updating your competitor analysis ensures that you stay ahead of the curve and can adapt swiftly to changes in the market.

. . .

IN IDENTIFYING MARKET GAPS, don't just focus on what's missing in terms of services or products. Consider gaps in customer experience, accessibility, convenience, and even community building. Sometimes, the differentiation lies not in what you offer but in how you offer it and how you make your clients feel.

IN CONCLUSION, understanding your competitors is not about imitating them but about learning what works, what doesn't, and where you can carve out a space that's uniquely yours. It's about understanding the battlefield in its entirety so that you can strategically position your fitness coaching business in a way that fills unmet needs and stands out. As you progress through this chapter, remember that competitor analysis is an ongoing process of learning, adapting, and innovating. It's about keeping your friends close and your enemies closer, not out of fear, but out of a desire to be the best in what you do.

Building a Business Plan

"A GOAL without a plan is just a wish." This insightful quote by Antoine de Saint-Exupéry perfectly encapsulates the essence of this chapter. Crafting a comprehensive business plan and setting clear, achievable goals are the bedrock of a successful fitness coaching business. As we conclude this exploration, let's dive into the essential components and strategies that will help you construct a solid business plan and set realistic goals for growth.

Crafting a Business Plan:

- **Market Analysis:** Assess the fitness industry landscape, understand current trends, and identify your target market.
- **Competitor Evaluation:** Research and analyze your competitors to identify gaps in the market.

- **Service Offering:** Clearly define your fitness coaching services, tailoring them to meet the needs of your target demographic.
- **Marketing Strategy:** Develop a plan for promoting your services, including digital marketing, community engagement, and partnerships.
- **Financial Planning:** Outline your expected revenue streams, startup costs, and budget for ongoing expenses.

Setting Goals:

- **SMART Goals:** Ensure your goals are Specific, Measurable, Achievable, Relevant, and Time-bound.
- **Short-term and Long-term Goals:** Balance immediate objectives with your vision for the future.
- **Adaptability:** Stay flexible and adjust your goals as your business grows and the market evolves.

Real-World Scenarios:

- **New Fitness Coach:** A new coach uses market analysis to identify a niche in offering online wellness coaching, sets initial goals to build an online presence, and outlines a financial plan considering limited initial resources.
- **Established Gym Owner:** An existing gym owner reevaluates their business plan, focusing on incorporating new trends like holistic health classes and sets goals for expanding their clientele base.

Perform Market Analysis:

- Conduct surveys and research to understand client needs.
- Analyze fitness industry reports for trends.

Evaluate Competitors:

- Visit competitor facilities and review their offerings.
- Identify areas where your services can stand out.

Define Services:

- List your coaching services and how they meet client needs.
- Consider unique offerings like nutrition advice or virtual coaching.

Develop a Marketing Strategy:

- Create a digital marketing plan.
- Engage in community events and build partnerships.

Outline Financial Plan:

- Calculate initial costs and expected revenue.
- Prepare a budget for marketing and operational expenses.

Set SMART Goals:

- Write specific and measurable short-term goals, like gaining 50 new clients.
- Define long-term objectives, like expanding to a second location.

Monitor and Adjust Goals:

- Regularly review business performance.
- Be ready to adapt goals based on market changes.

Tools:

- **Mindbody:** For client and class management.
- **Google Analytics:** To track website and campaign performance.
- **QuickBooks:** For financial planning and tracking.

CRAFTING a comprehensive business plan and setting achievable goals are critical steps in turning your fitness coaching ambitions into a thriving reality. This chapter has provided you with the tools and guidance to navigate this process effectively. Remember, a well-thought-out plan and clear goals are your roadmap to success in the competitive world of fitness coaching. As you turn the page, carry with you the knowledge that with meticulous planning and goal-setting, your fitness coaching business has the potential to not only succeed but thrive.

Part 2: Establishing Your Brand

IN A WORLD where fitness is not just a passion but a lifestyle, the power to stand out lies in the unique imprint you leave – your brand. This section lays the groundwork for the art of crafting a distinctive brand identity in the fitness industry. It's about transforming your vision into a tangible, relatable, and inspiring brand that resonates deeply with your audience.

THE JOURNEY BEGINS with developing a unique selling proposition (USP) that sets you apart in the fitness world. It's the essence of what makes your approach to fitness unique – be it your training style, your holistic approach to wellness, or your innovative workout regimes. This uniqueness becomes the cornerstone of your brand, defining not just what you offer, but how you offer it.

NEXT, we dive into crafting a brand image that echoes the heart of your services. It's not just about logos and color schemes; it's about creating an experience that speaks to your target audience. Your brand image is a reflection of your philosophy, values, and the transformation you promise your clients.

YOUR FITNESS PHILOSOPHY is the soul of your coaching style. It's what guides your methods and shapes the experiences you create for your clients. In this section, we explore how to establish and articulate a philosophy that not only defines your approach to fitness but also attracts the clientele aligned with your vision.

COMMUNICATING your philosophy isn't just about what you say; it's about how you make people feel. It's about building a connection that goes beyond the physical aspects of training and touches upon their aspirations for health and wellness.

. . .

IN THE DIGITAL AGE, an online presence is your gateway to the world. Here, we discuss how to utilize digital platforms effectively to not only establish but also grow your brand. From creating engaging content to interacting with your audience, your online presence is an extension of your brand identity.

WE ALSO DELVE into the world of SEO strategies, essential for enhancing your online visibility. It's about ensuring that when people search for fitness guidance, they find you – not just as a service but as a solution to their needs.

LASTLY, the art of networking and forming strategic partnerships forms a crucial part of business growth. It's about creating a community that supports and amplifies each other's efforts. Whether it's collaborations with other fitness professionals or partnerships with related industries, these connections open doors to new opportunities and mutual growth.

IN SUMMARY, this section is designed to be a comprehensive guide to establishing a robust brand in the fitness industry. From creating a unique identity to leveraging digital tools and forming meaningful collaborations, each aspect plays a vital role in the growth and success of your fitness business. Here, we lay the foundation upon which you can build a brand that not only stands out but also stands for something – a brand that truly represents you and the impact you wish to create in the world of fitness.

Creating a Unique Brand Identity

IN THE BUSTLING world of fitness coaching, carving out a distinct brand identity is akin to planting a flag in uncharted territory. It's the process of distinguishing yourself in a landscape crowded with fitness professionals, each vying for attention. Your brand identity is more than a logo or a catchy slogan; it's the essence of your story, values, and the unique flavor of your approach to fitness and wellness.

IMAGINE A FITNESS COACH, let's call her Jenna. Jenna started her journey much like any other fitness professional, with a passion for health and a certification in personal training. However, Jenna knew that to make her mark, she needed to stand out. She observed that most gyms and fitness coaches in her city focused heavily on bodybuilding and weight loss. But Jenna's passion was different; she believed in holistic wellness, integrating mind, body, and spirit. This became the foundation of her unique selling proposition (USP).

DEVELOPING a USP in the fitness world involves digging deep into what makes your approach different. For Jenna, it wasn't just about the physical transformation. It was about creating a balance in life, reducing stress, and improving mental health through fitness. Her programs included yoga, meditation alongside traditional fitness routines, and she often incorporated wellness workshops. This holistic approach resonated with a demographic that felt overlooked in the traditional fitness scene – those seeking inner peace as much as physical strength.

CRAFTING a brand image is a strategic process. It starts with understanding your target audience. Jenna realized her services appealed to busy professionals suffering from stress and burnout. Her branding – from her website to her marketing materials – reflected this understanding. Calming colors, images of serene fitness environments, and testimonials from clients who had achieved not just fitness goals but also stress relief, painted a vivid picture of what Jenna offered.

· · ·

YOUR BRAND SHOULD SPEAK to the aspirations and needs of your target audience. It's about creating an emotional connection. When potential clients come across your brand, they should feel an instant alignment with their fitness and wellness goals. Whether it's through your website, social media, or promotional materials, every touchpoint is an opportunity to reinforce what you stand for.

ONLINE PRESENCE IS a crucial element of brand identity in today's digital age. Jenna used her social media platforms not just to showcase client transformations, but also to share tips on managing stress, balancing work and life, and the importance of mental wellness. Her blog featured articles on nutrition, the science of stress, and mindfulness. By consistently providing value beyond just fitness tips, Jenna established herself as an authority in holistic wellness.

NETWORKING AND PARTNERSHIPS also play a significant role in brand building. Jenna connected with local businesses that aligned with her brand – like health food cafes, wellness retreat centers, and corporate offices. She offered lunchtime wellness sessions at local businesses and collaborated with cafes to provide healthy eating workshops. These partnerships not only expanded her reach but also strengthened her brand's association with a holistic lifestyle.

IN CREATING YOUR FITNESS BRAND, remember that authenticity is key. Your brand should be a true reflection of your values, beliefs, and approach to fitness and wellness. It's not about following trends or mimicking successful coaches, but about finding what's true to you and sharing that with the world.

AS YOU EMBARK on this journey of building your brand identity, keep in mind that it's an evolving process. The fitness industry is dynamic, and so are the needs and preferences of your clientele.

Stay flexible, listen to feedback, and be willing to adapt. Your brand is a living, breathing entity that grows with you and your business.

IN SUMMARY, developing a unique brand identity in the fitness world involves understanding your unique selling proposition, knowing your target audience, crafting a resonant brand image, establishing a strong online presence, and forging strategic partnerships. It's about creating an emotional connection with your clients through a brand that authentically represents your approach to fitness and wellness. Remember, your brand is more than a business; it's a reflection of your personal journey and professional ethos in the world of fitness.

Developing Your Fitness Philosophy

WHAT SETS A TRULY impactful fitness coach apart from the crowd? It isn't just knowledge of exercise science or the ability to demonstrate perfect technique. The heart of distinction lies in a coach's fitness philosophy – a set of guiding principles and beliefs that shape their approach to training and wellness.

YOUR FITNESS PHILOSOPHY is the backbone of your coaching style. It's not merely about what exercises you teach, but why you teach them, and the broader impact you aim to have on your clients' lives. Let's explore how to establish and communicate this philosophy to not only attract the right clientele but to also create a lasting impact in their lives.

Establishing Your Fitness Philosophy

THE FIRST STEP IS INTROSPECTION. Consider what aspects of fitness and wellness you're most passionate about. Is it helping clients achieve physical transformations, fostering mental well-being, encouraging holistic health, or maybe a focus on athletic performance? Your core values in fitness and life will be the foundation of your philosophy.

FOR INSTANCE, if you believe fitness is as much about mental strength as physical, this belief will shape your training programs, client interactions, and even the marketing language you use. It's about creating an approach to fitness that aligns with your beliefs and resonates with a specific audience.

Translating Philosophy into Practice

ONCE YOU'VE ESTABLISHED your philosophy, the next step is to integrate it into every aspect of your business. This includes the types of programs you offer, your teaching methods, and how you interact with clients. For example, if your philosophy emphasizes mindfulness and mental health, you might incorporate meditation sessions into your programs, choose a calming environment for training, and use motivational techniques that focus on mental resilience.

YOUR PHILOSOPHY also determines how you assess client progress. Traditional metrics like weight and muscle mass might be complemented by factors like improved sleep quality, stress reduction, or enhanced self-esteem, depending on what your philosophy prioritizes.

Communicating Your Philosophy

COMMUNICATING your philosophy effectively is crucial in attracting the right clients – those who share or aspire to your values. Your marketing materials, social media content, and even the décor of your training space should reflect your philosophy.

. . .

FOR INSTANCE, a coach focused on sustainable, long-term health might use imagery and language that showcases diverse body types enjoying various activities, rather than only highlighting extreme fitness transformations. This not only sets clear expectations but also attracts clients who align with your approach.

The Power of Storytelling

ONE EFFECTIVE WAY TO communicate your philosophy is through storytelling. Share your journey, why you developed your philosophy, and how it has shaped your approach to fitness. Stories of how your philosophy has impacted your clients' lives can also be powerful. These narratives help potential clients connect with you on a personal level and see the real-world application of your philosophy.

Adjusting and Evolving

IT'S important to remember that your fitness philosophy isn't set in stone. As you grow as a coach and learn from your experiences, your philosophy might evolve. Stay open to new ideas and feedback from clients. This adaptability not only keeps you relevant in a changing industry but also shows your commitment to continuous improvement.

IN SUMMARY, developing and communicating your fitness philosophy involves deep self-reflection, integrating your beliefs into your practice, effectively sharing your philosophy to attract like-minded clients, and remaining adaptable. Your fitness philosophy is more than a set of principles – it's a way of connecting with clients on a deeper level, guiding them towards not just physical fitness, but overall well-being. This approach not only distinguishes you in a crowded field but also fosters a more fulfilling coaching experience for both you and your clients.

Building an Online Presence

YOUR DIGITAL FOOTPRINT speaks volumes about your brand and philosophy, often reaching audiences before you do. In this digital age, effectively utilizing online platforms and implementing strategic SEO (Search Engine Optimization) strategies are not just beneficial; they're essential for any fitness coach looking to establish and grow their brand.

YOUR ONLINE PRESENCE is your digital storefront. It's where potential clients first encounter your brand, services, and philosophy. Therefore, your digital platforms should be reflective of your brand identity and values. This includes having a professional website, active social media profiles, and engaging content that resonates with your target audience.

A WEBSITE ACTS as the central hub for your online activities. It should be visually appealing, easy to navigate, and informative. Include sections about your services, your fitness philosophy, client testimonials, and a blog to share insights and tips. This not only aids in establishing credibility but also serves as a resource for potential clients.

SOCIAL MEDIA PLATFORMS LIKE INSTAGRAM, Facebook, and YouTube are powerful tools for fitness coaches. They offer an opportunity to showcase your expertise, share client success stories, and engage with your audience. Regular posts, stories, and videos can help keep your audience engaged and interested in your services.

SEO Strategies for Enhanced Online Visibility

SEO IS crucial for improving your visibility on search engines like Google. It involves optimizing your website and content so that you rank higher in search results for specific keywords related to your fitness services.

START with keyword research to understand what your target audience is searching for. Tools like Google Keyword Planner can help you identify relevant keywords. Incorporating these keywords into your website's content, blog posts, and even social media can improve your search engine rankings.

ANOTHER KEY ASPECT of SEO is creating quality content. Search engines favor websites that provide valuable and relevant information. Your blog can be an effective tool here, offering fitness tips, nutrition advice, and insights into wellness trends. This not only helps with SEO but also establishes you as an authority in your field.

BACKLINKS ARE ALSO vital for SEO. These are links from other websites to yours. Having high-quality websites link to your content can significantly boost your SEO efforts. You can achieve this by guest blogging on reputable fitness websites, collaborating with other fitness professionals, and creating shareable content.

Measuring Your Online Presence

To UNDERSTAND the effectiveness of your online strategies, it's essential to track and analyze your performance. Tools like Google Analytics provide insights into your website traffic, audience behavior, and engagement levels. Regularly reviewing this data can help you refine your strategies and better target your audience.

Staying Current with Digital Trends

THE DIGITAL LANDSCAPE IS EVER-EVOLVING, with new trends and technologies emerging constantly. Staying up-to-date with these trends and adapting your strategies accordingly can give you a competitive edge. For instance, the rise of video content has made platforms like YouTube and TikTok essential for fitness professionals.

Engaging with Your Audience

FINALLY, building an online presence is not just about broadcasting your message; it's about creating a dialogue. Engage with your audience by responding to comments, answering questions, and encouraging feedback. This not only helps build a community around your brand but also fosters trust and loyalty among your audience.

IN CONCLUSION, establishing and growing your brand in the digital world requires a strategic approach to online platforms and SEO. By creating a strong online presence, consistently producing quality content, and engaging with your audience, you can enhance your visibility and credibility as a fitness coach. Remember, in the digital world, your online presence is often the first and most impactful impression you make on potential clients.

Networking and Partnerships

"ALONE WE CAN DO SO little; together we can do so much." Helen Keller's words ring particularly true in the context of leveraging networking and forming strategic partnerships in the fitness industry. The final section of this chapter focuses on the synergistic power of collaboration and community in elevating a fitness business to new heights.

Leveraging Networking for Business Growth

NETWORKING in the fitness industry is not just about exchanging business cards or adding connections on LinkedIn. It's about building meaningful relationships that can lead to mutual growth and opportunities. The key to successful networking is to approach it with a mindset of offering value, rather than just extracting benefits.

ENGAGE WITH PEERS at fitness seminars, workshops, and conventions. Participate actively in fitness forums and online communities. Remember, every interaction is an opportunity to learn, share knowledge, and potentially collaborate.

Forming Strategic Partnerships

STRATEGIC PARTNERSHIPS in the fitness industry can take various forms. It could be partnering with a local nutritionist to offer comprehensive wellness packages, collaborating with a sports apparel brand for mutual promotion, or joining forces with a corporate entity to provide exclusive fitness programs to their employees.

THESE PARTNERSHIPS ARE NOT JUST about broadening your client base; they're about enhancing the value you provide. For example, a partnership with a physiotherapist could add a layer of injury prevention and recovery services to your offerings, thereby attracting a wider clientele.

Keys to Successful Partnerships

THE SUCCESS of a partnership hinges on a few key factors:

- **Alignment of Values and Goals**: Ensure that your partner's business philosophy and objectives align with yours. This alignment ensures a smooth collaboration and a consistent message to your clients.

- **Clear Communication**: Establish clear lines of communication and define the terms of the partnership from the outset. This includes understanding each party's responsibilities, expectations, and the desired outcome of the partnership.
- **Mutual Benefit**: A successful partnership should be beneficial for both parties. Whether it's sharing resources, knowledge, or client bases, ensure that the collaboration brings value to both sides.

Measuring the Impact of Networking and Partnerships

To GAUGE the effectiveness of your networking efforts and partnerships, track metrics such as referral rates, client retention rates, and the overall growth in business revenue. Feedback from clients and partners can also provide valuable insights into the effectiveness of these collaborations.

Evolving and Adapting

THE FITNESS INDUSTRY IS DYNAMIC, and so should be your approach to networking and partnerships. Stay open to new ideas and opportunities. What works today may not work tomorrow, so be willing to adapt and evolve.

NETWORKING AND FORMING strategic partnerships are powerful strategies for growing your fitness business. They provide opportunities for learning, collaboration, and expansion that you might not achieve alone. Remember, the strength of your network and partnerships can be a significant determinant of your success in the fitness industry. So go out there, connect, collaborate, and watch your fitness empire grow.

Part 3: Legal and Financial Considerations

IN THE DYNAMIC world of fitness coaching, where passion meets profession, there's a vital undercurrent that often goes unnoticed yet is crucial for the sustenance and growth of your business – the realm of legal and financial considerations. This section of the book is dedicated to navigating these essential aspects, laying a solid foundation upon which your fitness coaching empire can securely stand and flourish.

STARTING a fitness coaching business is more than just understanding health and exercise; it's also about comprehending the legalities that govern the industry. From obtaining the necessary certifications to ensuring compliance with local business regulations, this segment sheds light on the legal framework that surrounds the fitness coaching profession. It's about empowering you with the knowledge to operate your business within the bounds of the law, thereby safeguarding your hard-earned reputation and assets.

FINANCIAL HEALTH IS as crucial to your business as physical health is to your clients. Establishing sound financial practices early on is pivotal. This includes choosing the right tools and software for efficient financial management, which can range from simple budgeting apps to more complex accounting systems. We delve into how these tools can help you track your earnings, manage expenses, and understand the financial pulse of your business.

IN AN INDUSTRY where physical activity and health are involved, understanding the importance of insurance and liability cannot be overstated. This part of the chapter discusses the different types of insurance policies available and helps you determine which ones best fit your business model. It's about ensuring that both you and your clients are protected, providing peace of mind and fostering a safe training environment.

FINALLY, we tackle one of the most critical aspects of running a fitness coaching business – pricing your services. Developing a pricing strategy that reflects your value and expertise, while also being competitive and profitable, is a delicate balance. This section aims to provide you with insights and strategies to price your services effectively, ensuring that your business thrives financially while continuing to attract and retain clients.

IN ESSENCE, this part of the book is designed to guide you through the less talked about, yet essential aspects of running a fitness coaching business. It's about building a strong, legally sound, and financially healthy foundation, so your passion for fitness and coaching can continue to grow and positively impact more lives.

Understanding Legal Requirements

NAVIGATING the legalities of starting a fitness coaching business is akin to mastering a complex exercise routine – it requires diligence, understanding, and precision. For aspiring fitness entrepreneurs, understanding and adhering to legal requirements is not just a necessity but a cornerstone for long-term success. This section provides an in-depth exploration of the crucial legal aspects to consider when setting up your fitness coaching business.

WHEN EMBARKING on your fitness coaching journey, the first step is to understand the legal framework within which you must operate. This begins with choosing the right business structure, be it a sole proprietorship, a partnership, or a corporation. Each structure has its implications for liability, taxes, and operational flexibility. For instance, a sole proprietorship is the simplest form but offers less protection of personal assets.

It's ALSO essential to secure the necessary business licenses and permits. The requirements can vary significantly depending on your location. This might involve a general business license from your city or county, and possibly additional permits if you plan to sell products or offer services like nutrition advice.

Navigating Legalities in Business Operations

ONCE THE BUSINESS is legally established, there are ongoing legalities to navigate. These include adhering to employment laws if you plan to hire staff. As a business owner, you need to be aware of minimum wage laws, overtime rules, and employee rights. It's not just about compliance but creating a fair and legal working environment.

ADDITIONALLY, there are specific legal considerations unique to the fitness industry. If your business model includes digital elements like online coaching or selling fitness programs, you need to ensure compliance with online business regulations. This involves understanding e-commerce laws, digital copyright laws, and ensuring your website complies with privacy policies and data protection regulations.

Ensuring Compliance with Regulations and Certifications

PERHAPS THE MOST critical aspect specific to fitness coaching is ensuring compliance with industry-specific regulations and certifications. This is a dual-fold path involving both business and personal certifications. On the personal side, it's imperative to hold a recognized certification in fitness training. This not only enhances your credibility but is often a legal requirement to ensure that you are qualified to offer fitness guidance.

ON THE BUSINESS SIDE, if your services include nutrition advice, you may need additional certifications, as many regions regulate who can legally provide dietary guidance. It's also important to stay updated with any changes in the health and fitness regulations that could affect your business operations.

FURTHER, compliance extends to the equipment and facilities you use. If you own or operate a physical location, it must meet specific health and safety standards. Regular inspections might be necessary to ensure that your facility complies with local safety ordinances, fire codes, and hygiene standards.

IN SUMMARY, navigating the legalities of starting a fitness coaching business involves a comprehensive understanding of various laws and regulations. From setting up your business structure to complying with industry-specific standards, each step is crucial in building a solid legal foundation for your business. Adhering to these legal requirements not only safeguards you from potential liabilities but also builds trust with your clients, paving the way for a successful and reputable fitness coaching career.

Setting Up Financial Systems

IN THE WORLD of fitness coaching, where your focus is often on the physical transformation of your clients, it's easy to overlook the backbone of your business - the financial system. This vital aspect of your enterprise is what keeps it running smoothly, much like a well-oiled machine. So, how do you establish sound financial practices and choose the right tools and software for efficient management? This section delves into these critical questions, offering insights and practical advice for fitness professionals.

Establishing Sound Financial Practices

THE FINANCIAL HEALTH of your business is not just about the money you earn; it's about how you manage it. Sound financial practices begin with understanding the basics - budgeting, tracking expenses, and forecasting income. It's about being as disciplined with your finances as you are with your fitness routines.

CONSIDER THIS: a fitness coach who neglects their financial health is akin to an athlete ignoring their diet. Both are crucial for peak performance. Budgeting is your financial diet plan. It helps you allocate resources effectively, ensuring you have enough to invest in high-quality equipment, marketing, and continuous education, all of which are vital for the growth and sustainability of your business.

Tools and Software for Efficient Financial Management

IN TODAY'S DIGITAL AGE, numerous tools and software can simplify financial management for your fitness coaching business. From basic apps that track income and expenses to more sophisticated software offering detailed financial analytics, the choices are plentiful. But how do you choose the right one?

THE KEY IS to assess your specific needs. Do you require something straightforward for tracking daily expenses, or do you need a comprehensive system that includes features like invoicing, tax preparation, and payroll management? The answer lies in understanding the scale and complexity of your business operations.

· · ·

For instance, if you're a solo fitness coach, a simple mobile app might suffice. But if you run a fitness studio with multiple employees, you might need a robust system that can handle more complex financial tasks.

Practical Steps for Financial Management

- **Record-Keeping**: Maintain accurate records of all financial transactions. This not only helps in monitoring the financial health of your business but also simplifies tax filing.
- **Budgeting and Forecasting**: Develop a budget and stick to it. Regularly forecast your income and expenses to anticipate future financial needs.
- **Utilizing Financial Software**: Invest in reliable financial software that suits your business size and needs. This could range from basic accounting software to more advanced systems offering a range of financial services.
- **Seeking Professional Advice**: Don't hesitate to seek help from a financial advisor, especially when it comes to complex financial decisions or tax-related matters.

In conclusion, setting up sound financial systems is not optional; it's a critical component of your business's success. By implementing efficient financial practices and utilizing the right tools, you can ensure that your fitness coaching business not only survives but thrives. It's about making sure that the financial health of your business reflects the physical health you promote to your clients. Remember, a financially healthy business is one that can continue to make a positive impact on the lives of its clients for years to come.

Insurance and Liability

In the realm of fitness coaching, the significance of insurance and liability cannot be overstated. This section of our book delves into the intricacies of these topics, providing fitness professionals with essential knowledge to safeguard their businesses.

Understanding the Importance of Insurance in Fitness Coaching

Insurance in the fitness industry is not just a formality; it's a crucial safeguard. It's akin to a safety net for a trapeze artist - you hope never to need it, but its presence is vital for peace of mind. As a fitness coach, you are entrusted with the physical well-being of your clients. Despite your expertise and caution, accidents can happen, and unforeseen incidents can occur. Insurance is your defense against the unexpected, protecting you from potential financial ruin due to lawsuits or claims.

Choosing the Right Insurance Policies

Navigating the world of insurance policies can be as daunting as a complex workout regimen for a beginner. However, just like fitness, with the right guidance, it becomes manageable. There are several types of insurance policies that fitness professionals should consider:

- **Professional Liability Insurance**: This covers claims arising from the services you provide. Whether it's a workout injury or a health issue allegedly caused by your training, professional liability insurance is your first line of defense.
- **General Liability Insurance**: This is broader and covers injuries or damages that occur on your premises. If a client slips in your studio or a piece of equipment malfunctions, general liability insurance steps in.

- **Product Liability Insurance**: If you sell any products, from supplements to fitness gear, this insurance protects against claims of product-related injuries or health issues.
- **Business Interruption Insurance**: In the event of unforeseen circumstances like natural disasters, this insurance helps cover lost income and expenses.

EACH OF THESE insurance types serves a unique purpose. Choosing the right combination is akin to customizing a workout plan - it should be tailored to fit your specific business needs.

Key Considerations for Insurance Policies

WHEN SELECTING INSURANCE POLICIES, consider:

- **Coverage Limits**: Ensure the coverage limits reflect the potential risks and size of your business.
- **Deductibles**: Be aware of the out-of-pocket costs before the insurance kicks in.
- **Specific Exclusions**: Understand what is not covered under the policy.
- **Reputation of the Insurer**: Opt for an insurer with a solid reputation and experience in the fitness industry.

Anecdote for Reflection

CONSIDER the story of a well-known fitness instructor who faced a lawsuit after a client sustained an injury during a session. Despite the injury being a result of the client's negligence, the lawsuit resulted in significant legal fees. Fortunately, the instructor's robust insurance coverage provided a financial lifeline, saving the business from potential bankruptcy.

As a fitness professional, your focus is on enhancing the health and well-being of your clients. However, neglecting the health of your business in terms of insurance and liability can lead to dire consequences. The right insurance policies act as a protective shield, allowing you to focus on what you do best - guiding others on their fitness journey. Remember, being insured is not just about protection; it's about professional responsibility and peace of mind.

Pricing Your Services

In the final segment of this chapter, we focus on the crucial aspect of pricing your services as a fitness coach. This is where your expertise, value, and business sustainability intersect. Developing an effective pricing strategy is essential, as it directly impacts your profitability and market competitiveness.

Developing a Pricing Strategy That Reflects Your Value

Imagine your fitness coaching service as a premium brand. Each session you provide is more than just a series of exercises; it's an experience, a transformation, a journey towards better health. Your pricing should reflect the value of this journey. The key is to find a balance between what your market can bear and the worth of your unique skills and experience. This isn't just about setting a price; it's about communicating the value you bring to your clients.

Factors to Consider in Pricing

When determining your prices, consider:

- **Market Research**: Understand your target market's ability to pay and what competitors charge for similar services.
- **Costs and Expenses**: Factor in your costs, including equipment, space rental, insurance, and continuing education.
- **Experience and Specialization**: More experience or a unique specialization can justify higher rates.
- **Client Results and Testimonials**: Demonstrable results and positive client feedback can bolster your value proposition.

Balancing Competitiveness with Profitability

FINDING the sweet spot where your prices are competitive yet profitable can feel like balancing on a tightrope. Too high, and you risk alienating potential clients; too low, and you undervalue your service, potentially harming your business's financial health.

Dynamic Pricing Strategies

CONSIDER DYNAMIC PRICING STRATEGIES, like offering different rates for peak and off-peak hours, or providing package deals. This not only caters to various client budgets but also maximizes your earning potential across different times and seasons.

REFLECT on the story of a fitness coach who initially undervalued her services. Despite having a full schedule, her income wasn't reflecting the hard work and value she provided. After a thorough market analysis and evaluating her unique qualifications, she confidently raised her rates. Not only did her clients stay, but she also attracted a clientele that valued her expertise, thereby enhancing her business's profitability.

The Role of Communication

EFFECTIVE COMMUNICATION about your pricing is critical. When clients understand the rationale behind your rates and the value they receive, they're more likely to appreciate and accept your pricing structure. It's not just about the price; it's about the value they perceive.

IN CLOSING, setting the right price for your fitness coaching services is a strategic decision that requires careful consideration of various factors. It's a reflection of your value, your market, and your business goals. By finding the right balance, you not only ensure your business's financial health but also affirm your worth in the eyes of your clients. Remember, your pricing strategy is a key component of your brand and a crucial determinant of your business's success in the competitive world of fitness coaching.

Techniques and Process

Part 1: Assessing the Market

ANALYZING FITNESS INDUSTRY Trends

- Identifying current and emerging trends in fitness.
- Leveraging trends to find your unique fitness coaching position.

UNDERSTANDING CLIENT DEMOGRAPHICS

- Profiling potential clients: needs, preferences, and spending habits.
- Tailoring your fitness services to meet client demographics.

COMPETITOR ANALYSIS

- Researching and understanding your competitors.
- Identifying gaps in the market for unique positioning.

BUILDING a Business Plan

- Crafting a comprehensive business plan for fitness coaching.
- Setting clear, achievable goals for business growth.

Part 2: Establishing Your Brand

CREATING a Unique Brand Identity

- Developing a unique selling proposition (USP) in the fitness world.
- Crafting a brand image that resonates with your target audience.

DEVELOPING Your Fitness Philosophy

- Establishing a fitness philosophy that defines your coaching style.
- Communicating your philosophy to attract the right clientele.

BUILDING an Online Presence

- Utilizing digital platforms to establish and grow your brand.
- Implementing SEO strategies for enhanced online visibility.

NETWORKING AND PARTNERSHIPS

- Leveraging networking for business growth.
- Forming strategic partnerships in the fitness industry.

Part 3: Legal and Financial Considerations

. . .

Understanding Legal Requirements

- Navigating the legalities of starting a fitness coaching business.
- Ensuring compliance with regulations and certifications.

Setting Up Financial Systems

- Establishing sound financial practices for business health.
- Tools and software for efficient financial management.

Insurance and Liability

- Understanding the importance of insurance in fitness coaching.
- Choosing the right insurance policies to protect your business.

Pricing Your Services

- Developing a pricing strategy that reflects your value.
- Balancing competitiveness with profitability.

Action Item Checklist

PERFORM MARKET ANALYSIS:

- Research fitness trends and client preferences.
- Use tools like Google Keyword Planner for SEO.

Evaluate Competitors:

- Visit and review competitor facilities and offerings.
- Identify unique selling points for your services.

Define Services:

- List and describe your coaching services.
- Consider integrating nutrition advice or virtual coaching.

Develop a Marketing Strategy:

- Create digital marketing plans and community engagement initiatives.

Outline Financial Plan:

- Calculate start-up costs, expected revenue, and operational expenses.

Set SMART Goals:

- Define specific short-term and long-term business objectives.

Monitor and Adjust Goals:

- Regularly review business performance and adapt goals as needed.

Resource List:

TOOLS:

- **Mindbody:** For client management and class scheduling.
- **Google Analytics:** To monitor website performance.
- **QuickBooks:** For financial tracking and management.

BOOKS AND READING MATERIAL:

- **"The Lean Startup" by Eric Ries:** Strategies for efficient business planning.
- **"Building a StoryBrand" by Donald Miller:** Insights on creating compelling marketing strategies.

ADDITIONAL RESOURCES:

- **Online Courses:** Platforms like Coursera for business and marketing courses.
- **Professional Consultants:** Contact details for industry-specific business consultants.

designing profitable
fitness programs

. . .

IN THE EXHILARATING realm of fitness coaching, creating programs that not only transform lives but also drive business success is akin to crafting a perfect recipe – it requires a balance of ingredients, tailored to taste, yet universally appealing. Imagine the challenge of concocting a dish that delights every palate while maintaining the essence of your culinary art. This mirrors the art and science of designing fitness programs that cater to diverse client needs while ensuring your business thrives.

ENVISION A BRIDGE CONNECTING two cliffs - on one side, the varied aspirations and requirements of your clients, and on the other, the goals and objectives of your fitness coaching business. The creation of fitness programs that serve as this bridge is a dynamic and intricate process. It involves understanding the unique fitness journeys of your clients, recognizing their individual goals – be it weight loss, muscle gain, improved flexibility, or enhanced endurance. Simultaneously, it's about aligning these personalized programs with your business objectives, ensuring they not only deliver results to clients but also contribute to the growth and sustainability of your coaching venture.

. . .

THE JOURNEY ahead in this chapter unfolds an exploration of this delicate balancing act. We delve into the heart of fitness program creation, unraveling techniques to tailor routines that resonate deeply with client goals while weaving in strategies that bolster your business. It's about transcending the traditional approach of one-size-fits-all and embracing a philosophy where each client's success story contributes to the narrative of your business's triumph.

IN THIS EXPLORATION, we are not just discussing workouts and routines. We are talking about crafting experiences that leave a lasting impact on clients, experiences that they cherish, advocate for, and keep coming back to. It's a journey where every step, every leap, and every sprint is measured not just in calories burned or muscles toned, but in smiles earned, confidence gained, and lives transformed.

REMEMBER, your role as a fitness coach extends beyond the gym floors. You are a catalyst for change, a builder of dreams, and a guardian of health. Balancing client needs with business objectives is not just a skill; it's an art — an art that you are about to master.

Part 1: Program Development

Understanding Client Needs

IN THE BUSTLING world of fitness, the key to creating impactful programs lies not just in the exercises but in understanding the people who perform them. Picture a fitness coach, let's call her Emily, who begins her day not by planning workouts, but by diving deep into the lives and dreams of her clients. Her approach, rooted in empathy and understanding, transforms standard fitness routines into powerful tools for personal transformation. This narrative sets the stage for our exploration into the art of understanding client needs, a journey beyond mere physical training into the realm of personalized care and guidance.

THE PROCESS BEGINS with assessing client goals and fitness levels. Emily's first step with any new client is to conduct a detailed assessment, not just of their physical capabilities but of their lifestyle, habits, and deepest motivations. Imagine a client, Tom, who comes to her with the goal of losing weight. Through careful conversation, Emily discovers that Tom's real drive is not just to shed pounds but to regain the energy and confidence he once had. This revelation steers her program design in a direction far more attuned to Tom's true aspirations.

CUSTOMIZING programs to suit individual client needs is more than just adjusting the number of reps or the choice of exercises. It's about creating a journey that resonates with each client's unique story. Take another client of Emily's, Sarah, a busy mother of two, who struggles to find time for herself. Emily crafts a program for Sarah that integrates fitness into her daily routine, turning everyday activities into opportunities for exercise. This level of customization requires a deep understanding of a client's daily life, challenges, and joys.

. . .

However, this approach comes with its complexities. Balancing individual client needs with the broader objectives of a fitness business is akin to a tightrope walk. Emily must ensure that each personalized program not only satisfies her clients but also aligns with her business goals. It's a delicate balance of delivering results and driving revenue, where success is measured not just in financial terms but in the smiles and thank-yous of clients who feel seen, heard, and valued.

Throughout this section, we delve into the strategies and methods that enable fitness professionals like Emily to excel in understanding and meeting client needs. We explore how to conduct effective assessments, interpret client feedback, and translate this understanding into tailored fitness programs. The aim is to provide you, the reader, with the tools and knowledge to replicate this success in your own fitness coaching career.

By the end of this section, the concept of understanding client needs will transform from a theoretical idea to a practical skill set, empowering you to create fitness programs that are as unique as the individuals who follow them. You will be equipped to navigate the intricate dance of aligning personal goals with business objectives, ensuring that each step forward benefits both your clients and your coaching practice. This is not just about building a successful business; it's about forging a path that enriches lives, one personalized fitness program at a time.

Incorporating Diverse Training Modalities

Have you ever wondered why a fitness routine that works wonders for one person might not yield the same results for another? The answer lies in the diversity of training modalities. Diverse training methods not only cater to different body types and fitness goals but also keep clients engaged and excited about their fitness journey. This section of our exploration delves into the fascinating world of various training methods and how they can be adapted to spice up fitness programs, ensuring both variety and effectiveness.

THE WORLD of fitness is as varied as the people it serves. From the high-energy bursts of HIIT (High-Intensity Interval Training) to the serene flow of yoga, the range of training modalities available today is vast. Each modality comes with its unique benefits. For instance, weight training is excellent for building strength and muscle mass, while aerobic exercises like running or cycling are superb for cardiovascular health. But the magic happens when these modalities are combined in a well-rounded fitness program.

TAKE, for example, a client named John, who came to his fitness coach with the goal of losing weight. Initially, his program focused heavily on cardio exercises. However, after a few weeks, John's progress plateaued. His coach then introduced strength training into his routine. This shift not only reinvigorated John's enthusiasm but also accelerated his weight loss, as the combination of cardio and strength training proved more effective than cardio alone.

ADAPTING training modalities to suit individual client needs is both an art and a science. It requires a deep understanding of how different bodies respond to various exercises and an awareness of the latest research in fitness science. A fitness coach needs to be adept at identifying which combination of training methods will work best for each client. This could mean blending Pilates with sprint training for someone seeking to improve core strength and speed, or combining yoga with weightlifting for someone looking to increase flexibility and muscle tone.

THIS ADAPTABILITY also plays a crucial role in enhancing client engagement. Let's consider a case study of a fitness group where members were starting to lose interest. The coach introduced a mix of unconventional training methods like dance cardio and aqua fitness. This not only brought a refreshing change but also rekindled the group's enthusiasm, as members found new joy in these novel, fun activities.

INCORPORATING diverse training modalities is not without its challenges. It requires continuous learning and staying updated with the latest trends and scientific findings in fitness. Coaches must also be skilled in safely and effectively teaching these diverse methods, ensuring that clients enjoy their workouts without the risk of injury.

AS WE PROGRESS through this section, we will explore in-depth various training modalities, their benefits, and how they can be woven into a cohesive fitness program. From traditional methods like resistance training and cardio to more modern approaches like functional fitness and mind-body practices, we will provide you with the knowledge and tools to diversify your training programs effectively.

THIS EXPLORATION IS MORE than just an accumulation of exercises; it's about creating a symphony of movements that resonates with the unique rhythm of each client. By the end of this section, you will have a richer understanding of how to mix and match training modalities not only to achieve desired fitness outcomes but also to keep your clients engaged and motivated on their fitness journey. Remember, diversity in training is not just about variety; it's about crafting a personalized fitness experience that keeps clients coming back for more.

Creating Scalable Programs

"GIVE A MAN A FISH, and you feed him for a day. Teach a man to fish, and you feed him for a lifetime." This timeless proverb aptly encapsulates the essence of creating scalable fitness programs.

Designing a fitness regime that can be adjusted for different groups not only broadens its appeal but also lays the foundation for a sustainable, revenue-generating business model. This section delves into strategies for crafting scalable fitness programs, focusing on maximizing their impact and revenue potential.

SCALABILITY IN FITNESS programming is about creating a blueprint that can be modified to fit various client groups - from beginners to advanced athletes, from young adults to seniors. The challenge lies in designing a program flexible enough to cater to different fitness levels and goals, yet structured enough to maintain its core principles and effectiveness.

THE KEY to scalability lies in understanding the common denominators of fitness needs across different groups. For instance, regardless of their fitness level, most individuals benefit from a mix of cardiovascular, strength, and flexibility training. A scalable program might start with these basic elements and then introduce variations and intensifications to suit different levels of fitness.

CONSIDER the case of a fitness coach who designed a 12-week workout program aimed at improving overall fitness. The program was a hit among a wide range of clients, thanks to its flexible structure. For beginners, the focus was on mastering the basics and building endurance. Intermediate clients worked on enhancing their strength and stamina, while advanced clients tackled more challenging workouts that included high-intensity interval training (HIIT) and complex movements.

ONE EFFECTIVE STRATEGY for scaling your programs is the tiered approach. This involves creating different levels within the same program, each with increasing complexity and intensity. Clients can progress through these levels at their own pace, ensuring continuous challenge and engagement. For instance, a tiered weight training program might start with bodyweight exercises for beginners, progress to light free weights for intermediates, and advance to heavy lifting for experienced clients.

ANOTHER STRATEGY IS the modular design. Here, the program is divided into modules, each focusing on a specific aspect of fitness, such as cardio, strength, or flexibility. Clients can mix and match these modules based on their individual needs and goals. This approach not only provides customization but also keeps the program dynamic and interesting.

INCORPORATING technology can also play a significant role in scaling your fitness programs. Online platforms and apps allow for the distribution of tailored workout plans to a broader audience, enabling remote coaching and tracking of client progress. This digital approach opens up new revenue streams, reaching clients who may not be able to attend in-person sessions.

THE SCALABILITY of a fitness program also hinges on its ability to be delivered efficiently without compromising quality. Group classes, for example, can be an effective way to reach more clients at once, but they require skillful management to ensure that each participant's needs are met. This might involve having assistant coaches or utilizing fitness technology to provide personalized feedback within a group setting.

IT'S crucial to understand that scalability does not mean a one-size-fits-all approach. The goal is to create a core program structure that is adaptable and can be personalized to some extent. This personalization is key to keeping clients engaged and committed to their fitness journey.

. . .

IN CONCLUSION, creating scalable fitness programs is a balancing act between standardization and customization. It requires a deep understanding of different fitness levels, innovative program design, and efficient delivery methods. By mastering this balance, fitness coaches can maximize their impact, reaching a wider audience, and tapping into new revenue opportunities. In this section, we will explore in-depth the strategies and best practices for designing scalable fitness programs that meet the diverse needs of your clients while also driving your business forward.

Innovative Program Design

"INNOVATION IS the ability to see change as an opportunity - not a threat," said Steve Jobs, a sentiment that perfectly encapsulates the importance of innovative program design in the fitness industry. This final section of our chapter delves into the world of innovative techniques and technology in fitness program design, exploring how staying ahead of the curve with cutting-edge trends not only enhances client engagement but also propels your fitness business into the future.

INNOVATION IN FITNESS programming is all about thinking outside the box and embracing new methodologies. One such approach is gamification, which involves integrating game-like elements into fitness routines. This technique is especially effective in boosting motivation and engagement, turning mundane workouts into exciting challenges. For instance, incorporating a point system for completed workouts or setting up friendly competitions among clients can create a more interactive and enjoyable fitness experience.

ANOTHER INNOVATIVE TECHNIQUE is the use of virtual and augmented reality (VR/AR) in workouts. These technologies can transport clients to virtual environments, making exercises more immersive. Imagine cycling classes where participants can virtually ride through different landscapes, or yoga sessions that take place in calming, digital forests. VR/AR not only makes workouts more engaging but also accessible to those who prefer exercising in the comfort of their homes.

Integrating Technology in Program Design

INCORPORATING technology in program design is not just a trend; it's a necessity in today's digital age. Wearable fitness technology, like smartwatches and fitness trackers, has revolutionized the way we monitor and analyze physical activity. By integrating these devices into your fitness programs, you can offer personalized feedback based on real-time data, tailoring workouts to individual needs more effectively.

ADDITIONALLY, fitness apps have opened up new avenues for program delivery. They offer features like workout tracking, virtual coaching, and social sharing, which can significantly enhance the client's experience. For instance, developing a branded app for your fitness business can provide clients with easy access to workout routines, nutritional guides, and progress tracking, all in one place.

Staying Ahead with Cutting-Edge Fitness Trends

TO STAY AHEAD in the fitness industry, it's crucial to keep abreast of emerging trends. One such trend is holistic wellness, which emphasizes the balance between physical, mental, and emotional health. Integrating practices like mindfulness, meditation, and stress management into your fitness programs can address this growing demand for a more comprehensive approach to health and well-being.

ANOTHER RISING trend is functional fitness, which focuses on exercises that mimic everyday activities, enhancing daily living. Incorporating functional fitness into your programs can appeal to a wide range of clients, from young athletes to older adults looking to maintain their independence.

Actionable Steps for Innovative Program Design

- **Embrace New Methodologies:** Regularly research and experiment with new workout techniques and trends. Attend fitness expos, subscribe to industry publications, and join professional networks to stay updated.
- **Leverage Technology:** Integrate wearable tech and fitness apps into your programs. Offer virtual reality workouts or develop an app that provides personalized fitness guidance.
- **Educate and Train Your Team:** Ensure your trainers and staff are well-versed in these innovative techniques and technologies. Regular training sessions can keep your team skilled and knowledgeable.
- **Gather Feedback:** Continuously seek feedback from your clients about these new approaches. Use surveys or informal chats to understand what works and what can be improved.
- **Monitor Trends:** Stay alert to emerging trends in the fitness industry. Adapt your programs to incorporate these trends in a way that aligns with your business model and client needs.

By implementing these strategies, you can design innovative fitness programs that not only cater to the evolving needs of your clients but also set your business apart in a competitive market. This section provides you with the tools and knowledge to creatively enhance your program offerings, ensuring they are not only effective but also exciting and forward-thinking.

. . .

REMEMBER, innovation in fitness programming is not just about following trends; it's about creating a unique experience that resonates with your clients and aligns with your brand. It's about being a leader in the industry, setting the pace for others to follow. As we conclude this chapter, take these insights and strategies, and use them to craft fitness programs that are not only ahead of their time but also deeply impactful and rewarding for your clients.

Part 2: Marketing Your Programs

Effective Marketing Strategies

"MARKETING IS TELLING the world you're a rock star. Content Marketing is showing the world you are one," wisely observed Robert Rose, capturing the essence of effective marketing strategies. In this pivotal section of our chapter, we explore the art of developing marketing campaigns that not only resonate with your audience but also capitalize on the power of digital marketing tools for broader reach. Our focus is on delivering tactical insights and actionable steps, ensuring you know precisely what to do and why it matters in the dynamic realm of fitness marketing.

Crafting Resonant Marketing Campaigns

THE KEY to successful marketing lies in creating campaigns that speak directly to the heart of your audience. Start by identifying your ideal client – understand their desires, challenges, and aspirations. For instance, if your target audience is working professionals, tailor your marketing messages to address their time constraints and health goals.

CONSIDER the story of a fitness studio that revamped its marketing strategy to focus on stress relief for corporate employees. By addressing a primary concern of their target audience, they saw a significant increase in engagement and conversions.

Utilizing Storytelling in Marketing

STORYTELLING IS a powerful tool in marketing. It transforms basic communication into an engaging narrative that captures attention. Share success stories of your clients, or narrate the evolution of your fitness philosophy. This approach builds an emotional connection and lends authenticity to your brand.

Digital Marketing Tools for Broader Reach

IN TODAY'S DIGITAL AGE, leveraging online tools is non-negotiable for expanding your reach.

- **Social Media Platforms:** Utilize platforms like Instagram and Facebook to showcase client transformations, share fitness tips, and engage with your audience. Tailor your content to each platform's strengths and audience.
- **Email Marketing:** Regular newsletters with valuable content can keep your audience engaged. Share workout tips, nutrition advice, and behind-the-scenes glimpses of your fitness journey.
- **Search Engine Optimization (SEO):** Optimize your website and blog content with relevant keywords to improve your search engine ranking, making it easier for potential clients to find you.

Developing a Content Calendar

ORGANIZING your marketing efforts with a content calendar is crucial for consistency. Plan your social media posts, blog articles, and email newsletters in advance. This ensures a steady stream of content and helps in effectively managing your marketing efforts.

Engaging with Your Audience

ENGAGEMENT IS the soul of digital marketing. Respond to comments, conduct live Q&A sessions, and create interactive content like polls or quizzes. This not only boosts your visibility but also fosters a sense of community around your brand.

Measuring and Adapting Your Strategies

UTILIZE tools like Google Analytics to track the performance of your marketing campaigns. Pay attention to metrics like website traffic, engagement rates, and conversion rates. Use these insights to refine your strategies and adapt to changing trends and audience preferences.

Actionable Steps for Effective Marketing

- **Understand Your Audience:** Conduct surveys or hold focus groups to gather insights into your clients' needs and preferences.
- **Utilize Storytelling:** Share client success stories and personal anecdotes to build a narrative around your brand.
- **Leverage Digital Tools:** Use social media, email marketing, and SEO to widen your reach.
- **Create a Content Calendar:** Plan your marketing activities for consistency and efficiency.
- **Engage with Your Audience:** Be active in responding and interacting with your audience online.
- **Measure and Adapt:** Regularly analyze the performance of your campaigns and be ready to adapt to new trends and feedback.

EFFECTIVE MARKETING in the fitness industry is about connecting with your audience on a personal level and utilizing digital tools to amplify your reach. It's about crafting a narrative that resonates, engaging genuinely with your audience, and constantly evolving your strategies based on performance metrics. By implementing these tactical insights, you can develop marketing campaigns that not only capture attention but also drive substantial growth for your fitness business.

Client Testimonials and Success Stories

HAVE you ever wondered how a single story can transform the perception of your fitness business? This section delves into the power of client testimonials and success stories, an often-overlooked yet potent tool in your marketing arsenal. These narratives do more than just tell; they demonstrate the tangible impact of your services, enhancing marketing credibility and attracting new clients.

The Power of Client Testimonials

TESTIMONIALS SERVE AS SOCIAL PROOF, reinforcing your credibility and trustworthiness. They're the voice of your satisfied clients, resonating with potential ones. But how do you effectively collect and use these testimonials?

- **Collection:** Encourage your clients to share their experiences. After achieving a milestone or at the end of a program, ask for their feedback. Make this process easy and accessible, perhaps through a simple online form or a casual video interview.
- **Authenticity is Key:** Authentic testimonials, unscripted and in the client's own words, are far more effective than overly polished ones. Encourage clients to speak freely about their journey, the challenges they faced, and how your program helped them.
- **Utilize Diverse Formats:** While written testimonials are valuable, consider diversifying. Video

testimonials can be particularly compelling, showcasing real people and their stories.

Crafting Success Stories

A WELL-TOLD success story can be a powerful marketing tool. It's not just about before-and-after photos; it's about the journey. Here's how to craft these stories:

- **Narrative Structure:** Begin with the client's initial challenges and goals. Describe their journey through your program, highlighting specific struggles and breakthroughs. Conclude with their achievements and how their life has changed.
- **Emotional Connection:** Focus on the emotional aspects of their journey. What did they feel at their lowest point? How did their triumphs feel? This emotional depth will create a stronger connection with your audience.
- **Details Matter:** Include specific details about their regimen, such as changes in their workout routines or diet. This adds authenticity and relatability.

Using Testimonials and Stories for Marketing

ONCE YOU HAVE these testimonials and stories, it's crucial to use them effectively.

- **Website and Social Media:** Feature them prominently on your website. Create social media posts that tell these success stories, perhaps as a series.
- **Email Campaigns:** Share these stories in your email newsletters. They can be particularly

motivating for current clients and intriguing for prospects.

- **Advertising:** Use snippets of these testimonials in your ads. A genuine statement from a satisfied client can be a powerful motivator for potential clients.

Consent and Ethics

ALWAYS GET consent before sharing a client's story or testimonial. Ensure they're comfortable with the information being shared publicly.

Measuring Impact

TRACK how these testimonials and stories affect your engagement and conversion rates. Use tools like Google Analytics to see how they're influencing your website traffic and social media insights to gauge engagement.

Actionable Steps:

- **Develop a System for Collecting Testimonials:** Create a straightforward process for clients to share their experiences.
- **Narrate Success Stories:** Focus on the emotional and detailed journey of your clients.
- **Diversify the Formats:** Use both written and video formats for testimonials.
- **Integrate into Marketing:** Feature these stories on your website, social media, email campaigns, and advertisements.
- **Consent and Ethics:** Always obtain permission and respect client privacy.
- **Measure and Adapt:** Use analytics to measure the impact and refine your approach based on the data.

. . .

LEVERAGING client testimonials and crafting success stories are not just about showcasing results; they're about building a narrative that resonates with potential clients, illustrating the transformative power of your services. These stories do more than sell; they inspire and motivate, turning your clients' successes into your most compelling marketing tool.

Utilizing Social Media Effectively

"SOCIAL MEDIA IS NOT JUST an activity; it is an investment of valuable time and resources." This quote encapsulates the essence of mastering social media platforms to effectively promote your fitness programs. In this era, understanding and utilizing social media platforms isn't just a bonus; it's a necessity.

Choosing the Right Platforms

WHEN IT COMES to social media marketing, not all platforms are created equal. Each has its unique audience and best practices. Let's explore which ones to focus on and why:

- **Instagram:** With its visual-centric approach, Instagram is ideal for showcasing transformations, workouts, and healthy meals. It's perfect for reaching a younger demographic interested in fitness and lifestyle improvements.
- **Facebook:** Offering a diverse user base, Facebook is excellent for building a community. Utilize features like groups and live videos to engage with your audience more personally.
- **YouTube:** As the second-largest search engine, YouTube is vital for long-form content like workout

videos, nutritional advice, and client testimonials. It's a great platform to establish authority in your niche.

- **LinkedIn:** Often overlooked in the fitness industry, LinkedIn can be a goldmine for B2B networking, especially if you're targeting corporate wellness programs.

Engaging Content Strategies

CREATING engaging content is key to your social media strategy. Here are some actionable steps to elevate your social media content:

- **Storytelling:** Share your clients' journey in a way that resonates with your audience. Tell real stories of transformation and perseverance.
- **Educational Content:** Post workout tips, nutritional advice, and health-related facts. This not only provides value to your followers but also establishes you as an expert in your field.
- **Interactive Posts:** Use polls, quizzes, and Q&A sessions to engage with your audience. This not only boosts engagement but also helps you understand your audience better.
- **Consistency and Scheduling:** Post regularly but maintain quality. Use scheduling tools to maintain a consistent online presence without getting overwhelmed.

Leveraging Analytics

UNDERSTAND and leverage analytics to refine your strategy:

- **Track Engagement:** Monitor likes, shares, comments, and direct messages to gauge what content resonates with your audience.
- **Audience Insights:** Use platform analytics to understand your audience demographics. Tailor your content to suit their preferences and behaviors.

Building a Brand Voice

YOUR SOCIAL MEDIA should reflect a consistent brand voice that aligns with your business values and resonates with your target audience. Whether it's motivational, educational, or inspirational, keep it consistent across all platforms.

Collaborations and Influencer Partnerships

COLLABORATE WITH INFLUENCERS and other businesses in the fitness industry. This can expand your reach and bring credibility to your brand.

Social Media Advertising

UTILIZE TARGETED advertising options available on these platforms. They can help you reach a broader audience and are particularly effective for promotions and special events.

Crisis Management

BE PREPARED to handle any social media crises. Respond promptly and professionally to any negative feedback or situations that may arise.

. . .

Effective utilization of social media platforms is not just about posting regularly; it's about creating meaningful, engaging content that resonates with your target audience, analyzing the results, and continuously refining your approach. It's about building a community, establishing trust, and ultimately guiding that community from your social media pages to your fitness programs. Your goal is to not just gain followers but to create advocates for your brand.

Building a Referral Network

"Your network is your net worth." This insightful quote perfectly encapsulates the essence of building a successful referral network. In the fitness industry, a robust referral network can be a game-changer, transforming the way you attract and retain clients. This section delves into the strategies for creating an effective referral program and networking tactics to expand your client base.

Creating a Referral Program

A well-structured referral program encourages word-of-mouth marketing, a powerful tool in the fitness industry. Here are the steps to create a referral program that works:

- **Design an Appealing Incentive Scheme:** Your clients need a compelling reason to refer your services. Offer rewards that are both enticing to the referrer and beneficial to the new client.
- **Simplify the Referral Process:** Make it easy for clients to refer your services. Whether it's a simple form, a referral card, or a digital platform, the process should be straightforward and hassle-free.
- **Regularly Communicate the Program:** Ensure your clients are aware of the referral program. Use

email newsletters, social media, and in-person conversations to keep the program top of mind.

- **Track and Measure the Results:** Use a system to track referrals and measure the effectiveness of the program. This data will help you fine-tune the program for better results.

Networking Strategies

EXPANDING your client base requires proactive networking strategies. Here's how to effectively network in the fitness industry:

- **Attend Industry Events:** Participate in fitness expos, workshops, and seminars. These events offer a platform to meet potential clients and other fitness professionals.
- **Collaborate with Local Businesses:** Partner with local businesses that share a similar client base, like health food stores or sports equipment shops.
- **Leverage Social Media:** Use platforms like LinkedIn to connect with industry professionals. Join fitness groups and contribute to discussions to raise your profile.
- **Offer Guest Speaking or Workshops:** Position yourself as an expert by offering to speak at events or conduct workshops. This increases your visibility and credibility.

Crafting Success Stories

SUCCESS STORIES ARE a powerful tool in your marketing arsenal. They not only showcase the effectiveness of your programs but also inspire and attract new clients. Here's how to craft compelling success stories:

- **Gather Genuine Testimonials:** Encourage satisfied clients to share their experiences. Authenticity in these stories resonates more with potential clients.
- **Use Before and After Data:** Visual transformations are impactful. Combine these with data like improved fitness metrics to add substance to the stories.
- **Share Across Multiple Platforms:** Utilize your website, social media, and email newsletters to share these success stories, maximizing their reach.

Fostering Long-Term Relationships

BUILDING a referral network is not just about gaining new clients; it's about fostering long-term relationships. Keep in touch with your network through regular updates, appreciation events, and by offering continued value.

A REFERRAL NETWORK is an invaluable asset in the fitness industry. By creating a strategic referral program, actively networking, sharing success stories, and fostering long-term relationships, you can significantly expand your client base. This approach not only enhances your business growth but also contributes to building a community around your brand. Remember, the strength of your network is a reflection of your commitment to building and nurturing relationships.

Part 3: Program Delivery and Evaluation

Delivering Engaging Sessions

IMAGINE THIS: a fitness coach starts a session not by diving straight into the workout but by sharing a personal story of triumph over a fitness challenge. This not only captures the attention of the clients but also sets a tone of motivation and connection. This approach exemplifies a key aspect of delivering engaging sessions – the art of balancing professionalism with personal connection, and employing techniques that keep clients motivated and engaged.

Engagement Through Storytelling

STORYTELLING IS A POWERFUL TOOL. When a coach shares relatable experiences, it creates a bond of trust and inspiration. It's about striking the right balance – maintaining professionalism while being approachable and empathetic. Here's how to do it:

- **Share Relevant Personal Experiences:** When applicable, share your own fitness journey or challenges you've overcome. This can inspire and motivate clients.
- **Incorporate Client Success Stories:** Share anonymous stories of other clients' successes to motivate current clients, showing them what's possible.

Dynamic Session Planning

ENGAGEMENT IS NOT JUST about what you say, but also what you do. Dynamic session planning is key.

. . .

- **Variety in Workouts:** Keep the sessions fresh and exciting by introducing new exercises or variations. This prevents monotony and keeps clients curious about what's next.
- **Interactive Elements:** Introduce interactive elements like challenges or friendly competitions to foster a sense of camaraderie among clients.

Emotional Intelligence in Coaching

UNDERSTANDING AND RESPONDING to the emotional needs of clients is crucial.

- **Read the Room:** Pay attention to the clients' mood and energy levels. Adjust the intensity and style of coaching accordingly.
- **Empathetic Listening:** Be an active listener. Understand clients' concerns and fears, and offer supportive feedback.

Incorporating Technology

LEVERAGE TECHNOLOGY TO enhance the training experience.

- **Fitness Apps and Trackers:** Encourage clients to use fitness apps or wearables. This allows for tracking progress and setting personalized goals.
- **Virtual Reality and Interactive Games:** Introduce elements of virtual reality or gamification for a fun and engaging workout experience.

. . .

Feedback Loops

FEEDBACK IS A TWO-WAY STREET. It's essential for continuous improvement and client satisfaction.

- **Regular Check-ins:** Have regular check-ins with clients to discuss their progress, challenges, and feedback on the sessions.
- **Adapt Based on Feedback:** Be open to changing your approach based on the feedback received. This shows clients that their opinions are valued.

The Power of Motivation

A COACH's words can be a powerful motivator. Use them wisely.

- **Positive Reinforcement:** Regularly acknowledge the efforts and improvements of your clients. Celebrate their milestones, no matter how small.
- **Goal-Setting Sessions:** Have dedicated sessions for setting and reviewing goals. This helps clients stay focused and motivated.

DELIVERING engaging sessions is about more than just the physical aspect of training. It's about creating an experience that is emotionally resonant, motivational, and personalized. By weaving in personal stories, varying workout routines, practicing empathetic coaching, using technology, providing continuous feedback, and motivating clients, you create an enriching environment that clients are excited to return to. Each session becomes more than just a workout; it becomes an experience that clients value and look forward to. Remember, the most successful fitness coaches are those who understand that they are not just instructing; they are inspiring.

Utilizing Technology in Coaching

How OFTEN DO we see technology revolutionizing entire industries, reshaping how we interact, learn, and develop? In the realm of coaching, the advent of cutting-edge technology has opened doors to uncharted territories of program delivery and client experience enhancement. The question is, how can coaches harness this digital power to elevate their services?

Embracing Technology for Enhanced Coaching

AT THE CORE of modern coaching lies the effective implementation of technology. It's not just about using digital tools; it's about integrating them seamlessly into your coaching methodology to bring out the best in your clients.

- **Choosing the Right Tools:** Begin by identifying the specific needs of your coaching program. Which aspects of your coaching could benefit from digital enhancement? Is it client communication, program tracking, or interactive learning?
- **Personalizing Client Experience:** Use technology to tailor your coaching to each client's needs. Apps that track progress, provide feedback, and adjust programs based on client performance can significantly enhance personalization.

Leveraging Apps and Software

APPS AND SOFTWARE are not just accessories; they are pivotal in creating an engaging coaching environment.

- **Fitness and Wellness Apps:** Introduce clients to apps that track physical activity, diet, and mental wellness. These tools keep clients engaged and accountable outside of sessions.
- **Virtual Coaching Platforms:** Platforms like Zoom or Skype have made remote coaching a reality. They allow for face-to-face interaction, making the coaching experience more personal and effective.

Utilizing Data Analytics

DATA IS king in the digital age. Effective use of data can transform the way coaching programs are structured and delivered.

- **Progress Tracking:** Use software that analyzes workout data to track client progress. This data can help in making informed decisions about future training plans.
- **Feedback and Adjustments:** Continuous data analysis allows for real-time feedback and program adjustments, ensuring that clients are always on the right track.

Enhancing Communication and Engagement

EFFECTIVE COMMUNICATION IS the backbone of successful coaching, and technology has made it more efficient than ever.

- **Instant Messaging and Emails:** Utilize platforms that allow for quick and easy communication with clients. This keeps the lines of communication open, fostering a stronger coach-client relationship.
- **Social Media Engagement:** Use social media platforms to create a community for your clients. Share success stories, tips, and motivational content to keep clients engaged and inspired.

Overcoming Digital Challenges

WHILE TECHNOLOGY OFFERS NUMEROUS BENEFITS, it also comes with its set of challenges.

- **Tech Literacy:** Not all clients may be comfortable with using digital tools. Provide guidance and training to help them navigate these technologies.
- **Maintaining Personal Touch:** Despite the digital medium, ensure that your coaching retains a personal and empathetic touch. Technology should enhance, not replace, the human element of coaching.

IN WRAPPING UP THIS EXPLORATION, it's clear that the thoughtful integration of technology in coaching can lead to remarkable improvements in program delivery and client experience. It's about leveraging digital tools to create a more engaging, personalized, and efficient coaching environment. By embracing technology, coaches can not only stay ahead in their field but also provide unparalleled value to their clients. As we move forward in this digital era, the fusion of technology and coaching will undoubtedly continue to evolve, offering even more exciting possibilities for both coaches and clients.

Feedback and Continuous Improvement

IN THE EVER-EVOLVING world of coaching and program development, the maxim "feedback is the breakfast of champions" resonates more profoundly than ever. The fourth part of this chapter delves into the critical role of feedback and continuous improvement in crafting programs that not only meet but exceed client expectations. By integrating feedback effectively, coaches can turn good programs into exceptional ones.

Harnessing the Power of Client Feedback

THE TRUE VALUE of any program is measured by its impact on the client. Feedback, therefore, becomes an indispensable tool.

- **Creating Effective Feedback Channels:** Establish multiple channels for feedback, such as surveys, interviews, and informal conversations. Ensure these channels are easily accessible and inviting for clients.
- **Active Listening:** When receiving feedback, practice active listening. This means not just hearing but understanding the client's perspective, concerns, and suggestions.

Incorporating Feedback for Program Improvement

FEEDBACK IS NOT JUST to be collected but acted upon. Here lies the art of transforming insights into tangible improvements.

- **Prioritizing Feedback:** Not all feedback will be actionable or relevant. Prioritize feedback based on its potential impact on the program's effectiveness and client satisfaction.

- **Implementing Changes:** When integrating feedback, be clear about the changes made. Communicate these changes to your clients to show that their input is valued and has led to real improvements.

Strategies for Ongoing Program Evaluation and Refinement

A STATIC PROGRAM is a stagnant program. Continuous evaluation and refinement are key.

- **Regular Review Sessions:** Schedule periodic reviews of your program. Assess its strengths, weaknesses, and areas for improvement based on client feedback and your professional judgment.
- **Adapting to Change:** Be open to evolving your program. This might mean adopting new methodologies, tools, or even changing the program structure based on emerging trends and feedback.

Balancing Feedback with Professional Expertise

WHILE FEEDBACK IS CRUCIAL, balancing it with professional expertise and judgment is essential.

- **Filtering Feedback:** Learn to filter feedback through your professional lens. Not all client suggestions will align with your program's core objectives or coaching philosophy.
- **Educating Clients:** Sometimes, feedback stems from misunderstandings or unrealistic expectations.

Use these moments as opportunities to educate clients about the program's rationale and objectives.

Documenting and Tracking Feedback

MAINTAIN A SYSTEMATIC APPROACH TO FEEDBACK.

- **Documentation:** Keep a record of all feedback received. This documentation can be a valuable resource for tracking changes, understanding long-term client needs, and identifying patterns.
- **Measuring Impact:** After implementing changes based on feedback, measure their impact. This can be done through follow-up surveys, client interviews, or by evaluating client progress.

IN SUMMARY, feedback and continuous improvement are not just about making changes to a program; they are about fostering a culture of openness, adaptability, and client-centered growth. By embracing feedback, coaches can create programs that are dynamic, responsive, and, most importantly, effective in meeting and exceeding client expectations. Remember, in the realm of coaching, the pursuit of excellence is a journey, not a destination. Through continuous feedback and improvement, this journey becomes a rewarding and transformative experience for both the coach and the client.

Measuring Program Success

"SUCCESS IN COACHING is not just about doing things right, but also about doing the right things," a renowned coach once stated. This profound insight anchors our exploration of measuring program success, a crucial aspect of any coaching venture. The concluding section of this chapter examines the intricacies of setting and measuring key performance indicators (KPIs) and analyzing program outcomes to inform future strategies.

Setting Key Performance Indicators (KPIs)

THE KEY to measuring success lies in establishing clear, relevant, and achievable KPIs.

- **Align KPIs with Goals:** Ensure that each KPI directly reflects the program's objectives. If the goal is to improve client fitness levels, KPIs might include workout frequency, intensity, or endurance metrics.
- **Make KPIs Measurable:** Each KPI should have a quantifiable aspect. Whether it's numerical targets or qualitative benchmarks, the ability to measure progress is crucial.

Analyzing Program Outcomes

EVALUATING outcomes is more than just looking at numbers; it's about understanding the story behind them.

- **Use Data Effectively:** Collect data methodically and analyze it to glean insights. Patterns in client progress or feedback can provide invaluable information for program refinement.
- **Client Success Stories:** Assess the impact of your program through client testimonials and success stories. These narratives can be powerful indicators of your program's effectiveness.

Incorporating Technology in Evaluation

LEVERAGE TECHNOLOGY TO streamline the process of measuring and analyzing KPIs.

- **Utilize Software Tools:** Many software tools are available that can track and analyze KPIs efficiently. These tools can provide real-time data, making it easier to adjust strategies promptly.
- **Embrace Digital Feedback Systems:** Implement digital platforms for feedback collection. This can enhance the ease and frequency of feedback, providing more data for analysis.

Continuous Improvement through Feedback Loops

CREATE a system where feedback leads to action, and action leads to improvement.

- **Regularly Review Feedback:** Schedule periodic reviews of client feedback. This can highlight areas of success and those needing improvement.
- **Implement Changes:** Use the insights gained from feedback to make informed changes in your program. This shows clients that their input is valued and leads to continuous program enhancement.

Strategies for Future Program Development

USE the insights gained from KPI analysis to shape future strategies.

- **Identify Trends:** Look for trends in the data that can inform future program development. For example, if clients consistently struggle with a particular aspect of the program, consider modifying that component.
- **Plan for Scalability:** Consider how the program can be scaled or adapted for different client groups based on the success metrics.

In summary, measuring program success is a dynamic and multifaceted process. It involves setting the right KPIs, using data effectively, leveraging technology, engaging in continuous improvement through feedback, and using these insights for future program development. By adhering to these principles, coaches can ensure their programs are not only successful but also continuously evolving to meet the changing needs of their clients. In the ever-changing world of coaching, the ability to measure and adapt is not just a skill but a necessity for sustained success.

Techniques and Process

Part 1: Program Development

Understanding Client Needs

- Assessing client goals and fitness levels.
- Customizing programs to suit individual client needs.

Incorporating Diverse Training Modalities

- Exploring various training methods for program diversity.
- Adapting training modalities to enhance client engagement.

Creating Scalable Programs

- Designing programs that can be scaled for different groups.
- Strategies for maximizing impact and revenue with scalable programs.

Innovative Program Design

- Incorporating innovative techniques and technology in program design.
- Staying ahead of the curve with cutting-edge fitness trends.

Part 2: Marketing Your Programs

EFFECTIVE MARKETING STRATEGIES

- Developing marketing campaigns that resonate with your audience.
- Utilizing digital marketing tools for broader reach.

Client Testimonials and Success Stories

- Leveraging client testimonials for marketing credibility.
- Crafting success stories that inspire and attract new clients.

Utilizing Social Media Effectively

- Mastering social media platforms to promote your programs.
- Engaging content strategies for social media marketing.

Building a Referral Network

- Creating a referral program to encourage word-of-mouth marketing.
- Networking strategies to expand your client base.

Part 3: Program Delivery and Evaluation

DELIVERING Engaging Sessions

- Techniques for engaging and motivating clients during sessions.
- Balancing professionalism and personal connection in coaching.

Utilizing Technology in Coaching

- Implementing technology for effective program delivery.
- Leveraging apps and software for enhanced client experiences.

Feedback and Continuous Improvement

- Gathering and incorporating client feedback for program improvement.
- Strategies for ongoing program evaluation and refinement.

Measuring Program Success

- Setting and measuring key performance indicators (KPIs) for success.
- Analyzing program outcomes to inform future strategies.

Understanding Client Needs

- **Example:** A fitness coach conducts a holistic assessment for a new client, including lifestyle, diet, and fitness goals. Tailored programs are then developed, like designing a low-impact routine for a client with joint issues.
- **Process:** Start with a detailed questionnaire, followed by a personal discussion to understand deeper motivations and challenges. Then, customize the workout plan to align with these insights.

Incorporating Diverse Training Modalities

- **Example:** For a client aiming for weight loss, blend cardio with strength training. For another seeking stress relief, combine yoga with aerobic exercises.
- **Process:** Assess the client's goals and interests. Introduce various training forms and observe their response. Gradually build a diverse yet cohesive program that targets their specific objectives.

Creating Scalable Programs

- **Example:** Develop a core training program that can be adjusted for different fitness levels, adding complexities like weight and intensity variations.
- **Process:** Identify common goals across various client groups. Design a flexible program structure that allows for modifications, ensuring it remains challenging and engaging for clients at different levels.

Innovative Program Design

- **Example:** Use gamification to make workouts engaging. Set up a points system for each exercise completion or a fitness challenge with leaderboards.
- **Process:** Stay updated on fitness trends and technologies. Regularly introduce new elements into the program, ensuring they align with clients' interests and goals.

Action Item Checklist:

Conduct Client Assessments:

- **Step 1:** Prepare a comprehensive questionnaire covering health history, fitness goals, and lifestyle.
- **Step 2:** Conduct a one-on-one session to discuss the questionnaire responses in depth.
- **Step 3:** Perform a physical assessment to gauge current fitness levels.

Develop Tailored Fitness Programs:

- **Step 1:** Based on the assessment, identify key focus areas for each client.
- **Step 2:** Design a workout plan incorporating exercises targeting these areas.
- **Step 3:** Integrate feedback from clients and adjust the plan as necessary.

Implement Diverse Training Modalities:

- **Step 1:** Research various training methods suitable for different goals.
- **Step 2:** Introduce these methods to clients, starting with basic techniques.
- **Step 3:** Gradually mix different modalities to keep the routines dynamic.

Design Scalable Fitness Programs:

- **Step 1:** Create a foundational program template.
- **Step 2:** Add variations for different skill levels.
- **Step 3:** Regularly review and update the program based on client progression.

. . .

INTEGRATE INNOVATIVE ELEMENTS:

- **Step 1:** Explore new fitness technologies and trends.
- **Step 2:** Gradually introduce these elements into your programs.
- **Step 3:** Gather client feedback on these innovations and make necessary adjustments.

Resource List

TOOLS:

- **MyFitnessPal:** For tracking diet and exercise.
- **Fitbit or similar wearables:** For monitoring physical activities and health metrics.
- **Zoom or Skype:** For conducting virtual training sessions.

BOOKS AND READING MATERIAL:

- "Strength Training Anatomy" by Frederic Delavier: Offers detailed insights into strength training exercises.
- "The Lean Startup" by Eric Ries: Provides valuable lessons on innovation and adapting to client needs.

ADDITIONAL RESOURCES:

- **Online Courses:** Websites like Coursera or Udemy offer courses on fitness training and business management.

- **Industry Experts:** Contact local fitness experts for insights and collaboration opportunities. Use platforms like LinkedIn for networking.

building a client base for your fitness business

. . .

IMAGINE your fitness business not just as a place for exercise, but a thriving community where every member feels valued and invested in. This vision is at the heart of Chapter 3, where we explore the vital elements of building and nurturing a client base for your fitness business. As a fitness professional, the growth and sustainability of your business hinge on your ability to attract, retain, and expand your client base. This chapter is dedicated to unfolding the strategies and practices that make this possible, balancing quality service with the overarching objectives of business growth.

IN THE FIRST part of this chapter, we delve into the art of attracting clients. It begins with identifying your ideal client – understanding who they are, what they seek, and how your services align with their goals. This understanding is critical in tailoring your marketing efforts to appeal directly to the people who will benefit most from your expertise. We then move on to explore various effective advertising techniques, emphasizing the importance of leveraging both online and offline platforms to reach a wider audience. This includes harnessing the power of social proof, such as client reviews and endorsements, which play a significant role in building trust and credibility. Additionally, the judicious use of promotions and discounts is discussed, focusing on creating offers that are both enticing for new clients and sustainable for your business's profitability.

THE SECOND PART of this chapter focuses on client retention strategies. Providing exceptional client service forms the core of this discussion, emphasizing personalized attention and exceptional service as key drivers of client satisfaction and loyalty. We also address the importance of client engagement and communication, highlighting effective techniques and the role of technology in maintaining ongoing communication. Adapting programs to meet evolving client needs and implementing progress tracking are also crucial for client satisfaction and will be examined in detail. Building a community around your brand is another strategic approach we explore, leveraging the power of a supportive and interactive client group to enhance loyalty and facilitate referrals.

IN THE THIRD PART, we broaden the scope to include strategies for expanding your client base. This involves exploring new markets and identifying opportunities to tap into different client demographics. Collaborations and partnerships with other fitness professionals and businesses are also discussed as a means to mutual growth and client base expansion. Hosting events and workshops is presented as a strategy not only for brand exposure but also as a platform for client engagement and acquisition. Lastly, the chapter will cover diversifying your offerings, balancing specialization with the introduction of new services or programs to attract a more diverse clientele.

THROUGHOUT THIS CHAPTER, the emphasis is placed on practical, actionable strategies that align with the core values of your fitness business. The goal is to equip you with the knowledge and tools necessary to not only attract and retain clients but to create a thriving fitness community that stands the test of time. This journey is about more than just numbers; it's about fostering relationships, understanding client needs, and continuously adapting to provide the best possible service. Let's embark on this path together, transforming your fitness business into a beacon of health, community, and growth.

Part 1: Attracting Clients

Identifying Your Ideal Client

IN THE BUSTLING heart of a vibrant city, there once stood a small, unassuming gym that transformed into a flourishing fitness hub. The secret? Its owner, Sarah, had mastered the art of identifying and appealing to her ideal client. This is where our exploration begins in understanding the critical importance of knowing exactly who your target clients are and how to tailor your marketing to resonate with them deeply.

SARAH'S JOURNEY wasn't without challenges. Initially, her gym catered to a broad audience, but it was struggling to grow. She realized the need for a more focused approach. The first step was defining the characteristics of her target client. Sarah conducted surveys and collected data, which revealed that her most loyal clients were working professionals in their 30s seeking a balance between a rigorous workout and a community feel. With this revelation, she began the pivotal task of tailoring her marketing efforts specifically to this group.

THE TRANSFORMATION DIDN'T HAPPEN OVERNIGHT. Sarah revamped her gym's branding, messaging, and services to align with the preferences of her ideal clients. She redesigned her website and social media to reflect a message that resonated with busy professionals looking for an efficient and welcoming workout environment. She emphasized the benefits of her services, such as time-efficient workouts and a supportive community, through targeted online advertising and engaging social media campaigns.

IN PARALLEL, Sarah tapped into effective advertising techniques. She explored a mix of online and offline strategies to broaden her reach. Online, she leveraged social media platforms, targeting ads specifically to local professionals. Offline, she engaged in community events and partnered with local businesses to offer exclusive deals, effectively reaching potential clients outside the digital sphere.

A CRUCIAL ELEMENT of her revamped strategy was leveraging social proof. Sarah encouraged her satisfied clients to share their experiences online. Positive reviews and client testimonials began to appear on her website and social media, adding a layer of trust and credibility. She also implemented a referral program, rewarding clients for bringing in friends, which not only increased her client base but also strengthened the community feel of her gym.

OFFERING promotions and discounts played a significant role in attracting new clients. However, Sarah was careful to balance these promotions with the long-term profitability of her gym. She offered well-thought-out introductory deals that were enticing yet sustainable, and these promotions were targeted to align with the interests and needs of her ideal clients.

THIS SECTION of our exploration emphasizes the importance of understanding your target audience and tailoring your marketing strategies accordingly. Sarah's story is a testament to the power of focused marketing and the impact it can have on business growth. It underlines the necessity of not just casting a wide net in the hopes of catching anyone but rather using a spear to precisely target those who will most benefit from and appreciate your services.

AS WE DELVE FURTHER, remember Sarah's story. It's a reminder that identifying and appealing to your ideal client isn't just about attracting any client; it's about attracting the right client. This approach leads to a more engaged client base, increased client satisfaction, and ultimately, a more successful and fulfilling business. The subsequent sections will build upon this foundation, providing you with comprehensive tactical insights and actionable steps to not only identify your ideal client but to engage and retain them, leading to sustainable business growth and success.

Effective Advertising Techniques

HAVE you ever pondered how some fitness programs seem to effortlessly draw in clients, while others struggle to get noticed? The secret often lies in their advertising techniques. This chapter section explores various effective advertising methods, emphasizing the importance of a well-rounded approach that combines both online and offline strategies for maximum impact. The focus is not just on attracting new clients but also on creating a lasting impression that ensures their continued engagement with your fitness programs.

Online Advertising: The Digital Frontier

ONLINE ADVERTISING HAS REVOLUTIONIZED the way fitness programs connect with potential clients. It's not just about being online; it's about crafting a digital presence that resonates with your target audience.

- **Social Media Marketing**: Platforms like Instagram and Facebook are invaluable for reaching a broad audience. Sharing client success stories, workout tips, and engaging content can create a community around your brand. Personalized responses to comments and messages help foster a sense of connection.
- **Search Engine Optimization (SEO)**: Optimizing your website with relevant keywords ensures higher visibility on search engine results pages. This tactic is vital for attracting individuals actively searching for fitness programs.

- **Pay-Per-Click Advertising**: Platforms like Google Ads offer pay-per-click advertising, where you can display ads in search engine results and only pay when someone clicks on your ad. This method is effective for targeting specific demographics or interests.
- **Email Marketing**: Building an email list and regularly sending out newsletters keeps your program top of mind. Share updates, fitness tips, and special offers to maintain engagement.

Offline Advertising: The Power of Personal Touch

WHILE THE DIGITAL world offers vast opportunities, offline advertising still plays a crucial role. It adds a personal touch that digital methods sometimes lack.

- **Community Events**: Participating in or hosting community events, like local marathons or health fairs, can increase your visibility. These events provide an opportunity to connect personally with potential clients and leave a lasting impression.
- **Flyers and Posters**: Strategically placed flyers and posters in local businesses, such as health food stores or community centers, can capture the attention of potential clients who may not be reached online.
- **Networking**: Building relationships with other local businesses and professionals can lead to referrals. For instance, partnering with a nutritionist or a physiotherapist can create a referral network that benefits all parties involved.
- **Word of Mouth**: Encouraging your current clients to talk about your program to friends and family can be incredibly effective. Offering incentives for referrals can motivate clients to spread the word.

. . .

Integrating Online and Offline Strategies

THE MOST SUCCESSFUL advertising approach integrates both online and offline strategies. This integration ensures a wide-reaching impact.

- **Promote Offline Events Online**: Use your social media platforms and email lists to promote upcoming offline events. This approach helps in reaching a broader audience and increases event attendance.
- **Online Follow-Ups to Offline Interactions**: After meeting potential clients at events, follow up with them online. Send them an email thanking them for their interest and providing more information about your program.
- **Consistent Branding Across All Platforms**: Ensure that your branding, message, and tone are consistent across all online and offline advertising platforms. This consistency helps in building a strong, recognizable brand.

IN TODAY's competitive fitness industry, relying solely on either online or offline advertising is no longer sufficient. A blend of both is essential for maximizing your reach and impact. By implementing these tactics, you can attract more clients and grow your fitness business more effectively. The key is to remain authentic, consistent, and engaged with both your current and potential clients. This chapter section provides a comprehensive guide on leveraging various advertising techniques, ensuring you have the tools needed to create a successful, multi-faceted advertising strategy for your fitness program.

Leveraging Social Proof

"Nothing draws a crowd quite like a crowd," P.T. Barnum once said, a sentiment that perfectly captures the essence of leveraging social proof in today's fitness industry. This section of the chapter delves into the art of using client reviews, endorsements, and testimonials as powerful tools to attract new clients and establish credibility.

In the realm of fitness and wellness, where personal experience and results speak louder than any sales pitch, social proof stands as a testament to the effectiveness of your programs. It's the bridge of trust that connects a potential client's uncertainty to a confident decision to join your program.

Harnessing Client Reviews and Endorsements

- **Gathering Reviews**: The first step is encouraging your existing clients to share their experiences. This could be done through post-session surveys, emails, or a quick chat at the end of a session. Make it easy and convenient for them to leave feedback.
- **Managing Online Reviews**: Websites like Google, Yelp, and Facebook are platforms where many potential clients first encounter your business. Regularly monitor these sites, respond to reviews (both positive and negative), and thank clients for their feedback. This not only improves your online presence but also shows that you value client input.
- **Video Testimonials**: There's something incredibly compelling about watching someone speak passionately about their transformation journey. Capture these stories on video and share them on your website and social media channels.

Implementing Endorsements in Marketing

- **Celebrity and Influencer Endorsements**: Collaborating with well-known personalities who can vouch for your program adds immense credibility. However, ensure that these endorsements are authentic and align with your brand values.
- **Client Success Stories in Marketing Materials**: Incorporate success stories and client testimonials in your marketing collateral. This could be in your brochures, email campaigns, or as part of your website's landing page.
- **Leveraging User-Generated Content**: Encourage clients to share their fitness journey on their social media and tag your program. Reposting these on your channels not only provides social proof but also builds community among clients.

Ethical Considerations and Authenticity

- **Maintaining Authenticity**: Always ensure that the reviews and endorsements are genuine. Fabricated or exaggerated claims can significantly harm your credibility.
- **Respecting Privacy**: Always seek permission before sharing a client's story or pictures, especially if it involves personal or sensitive information.

Tactical Application of Social Proof

- **Incorporate Reviews in Sales Conversations**: Train your sales team to use these testimonials and reviews as part of their pitch. Hearing or reading about someone's positive experience can be a powerful motivator for potential clients.
- **Regular Updates**: Continuously update the testimonials and success stories on all your platforms.

Fresh content keeps your marketing dynamic and relatable.

- **Highlight Diverse Experiences**: Show a range of success stories that cater to different demographics and fitness goals. This inclusivity can resonate with a broader audience.

EFFECTIVELY LEVERAGING social proof is about much more than just collecting and displaying positive reviews. It's about creating a culture where feedback is valued, shared, and used as a tool to attract and retain clients. By implementing these strategies, your fitness program can harness the power of social proof to not only enhance its marketability but also to build a community of motivated and loyal clients. Remember, in the fitness industry, the voices of your clients are your strongest advocates. Use them wisely and authentically, and they can be the driving force behind your program's growth and success.

Offering Promotions and Discounts

"DISCOUNTS AND PROMOTIONS are like spices; used right, they can create a masterpiece, but overdone, they can spoil the whole dish," a wise marketer once said. This analogy is particularly relevant in the context of fitness businesses, where the balance between enticing offers and maintaining profitability is crucial. In this final part of our chapter, we explore the art of designing promotions and discounts that not only attract new clients but also ensure the financial health of your business.

Creating Enticing Offers

- **Understand Your Audience**: Before launching any promotion, it's crucial to understand your target audience. What motivates them? Are they looking for short-term fitness goals or long-term health solutions?

Tailoring your offers to meet these needs can significantly increase their effectiveness.

- **Innovative Promotion Ideas**: Instead of just discounts, think creatively. Offer a free nutrition consultation with every membership, a complimentary fitness assessment, or a referral bonus. These value-added services not only attract clients but also enhance their overall experience.
- **Limited-Time Offers**: Creating a sense of urgency can encourage potential clients to act quickly. Limited-time offers, such as a discounted rate for the first 50 sign-ups or special prices during holidays, can create a buzz and drive immediate action.

Balancing Promotions with Profitability

- **Cost-Benefit Analysis**: Before rolling out any promotional offer, conduct a thorough cost-benefit analysis. Consider the potential long-term value of new clients against the immediate cost of the promotion.
- **Tiered Membership Options**: Offer different levels of membership, each with its own set of benefits and price points. This not only caters to a wider range of clients but also helps in maintaining profitability.
- **Tracking and Measuring Success**: Implement systems to track the performance of your promotions. Use metrics like client acquisition cost, retention rate, and overall revenue growth to assess the success of your offers.

Actionable Steps for Effective Promotions

- **Develop a Promotional Calendar**: Plan your promotional activities in advance. Align them with specific times of the year when people are more likely to join fitness programs, such as New Year's or just before summer.
- **Engage Through Social Media**: Use social media platforms to promote your offers. Eye-catching graphics, engaging content, and testimonials can significantly enhance the visibility of your promotions.
- **Personalized Email Marketing**: Send personalized emails to your existing and potential clients with details of your offers. Use segmentation to tailor your messages to different audience groups.
- **Feedback and Adaptation**: After the promotion ends, gather feedback from clients. What did they like or dislike about the offer? Use this information to refine future promotions.

REMEMBER THAT PROMOTIONS AND DISCOUNTS, when used judiciously, can be powerful tools to expand your client base and strengthen your fitness business. The key is to strike the right balance, ensuring that these offers attract clients in a way that contributes positively to your business's bottom line. By following the strategies and actionable steps outlined above, you can create promotions that are not only enticing but also sustainable and profitable.

STANDING out requires not just excellent services, but also smart marketing and promotional strategies. By mastering the art of offering promotions and discounts, you position your business for growth and success, creating a win-win situation for both your clients and your business.

Part 2: Client Retention Strategies

Providing Exceptional Client Service

IN THE REALM OF FITNESS, exceptional client service isn't just about guiding someone through a workout; it's about crafting an experience that resonates on a personal level, fostering trust and loyalty. This segment delves into the nuances of providing exceptional service and building strong, lasting relationships with clients.

Creating Personalized Client Experiences

- **Understanding Individual Needs**: Begin by recognizing that each client comes with unique goals, preferences, and challenges. This understanding forms the bedrock of personalized attention. For instance, consider a client like Sarah, a working mother, whose fitness plan might include exercises that can be seamlessly integrated into her busy schedule.
- **Customization of Services**: Tailor your services to meet these individual needs. It's not just about custom workout plans, but also about how you interact with each client. For instance, some clients might prefer more encouragement and feedback, while others might value a more data-driven approach.
- **Continuous Adaptation**: As your clients evolve, so should your services. Regular check-ins and adaptability in your training plans can significantly enhance client satisfaction. For example, as a client progresses, gradually introduce more challenging workouts or new activities to keep them engaged.

Building Strong, Lasting Relationships

- **Effective Communication**: Foster open lines of communication. Regular updates, feedback sessions, and being accessible for queries can build trust and a sense of being valued. Remember, effective communication is not just about speaking but also about listening.
- **Building a Community**: Create a sense of community among your clients. Encourage interaction through group classes, social events, or online forums. For instance, organizing a monthly group hike can provide a platform for clients to connect outside the gym.
- **Recognition and Appreciation**: Acknowledge milestones and achievements. This recognition can be as simple as a congratulatory message for reaching a fitness goal or celebrating a client's workout anniversary.

Ensuring Client Retention

- **Consistent Quality**: Ensure that the quality of your service remains consistently high. This includes everything from the cleanliness of your facility to the standard of your training sessions.
- **Adding Value**: Continuously look for ways to add value to your clients' experience. This could be through educational workshops, nutrition counseling, or bringing in guest speakers on topics of interest.
- **Feedback Loop**: Implement a system for regular feedback. Use this feedback to make improvements and show your clients that their opinions matter.

Actionable Steps for Enhancing Client Service

- **Develop a Client Profile System**: Create detailed profiles for each client, including their fitness goals, preferences, and feedback. Regularly update these profiles.
- **Implement Customized Training Plans**: Based on these profiles, develop individualized training plans that cater to each client's specific needs.
- **Schedule Regular Check-ins**: Set up monthly or quarterly meetings to discuss progress, challenges, and any adjustments needed in their training plan.
- **Organize Community Events**: Plan regular events or activities that encourage client interaction and foster a sense of community.
- **Celebrate Achievements**: Recognize and celebrate client milestones, both big and small. This can be done through social media shoutouts, in-person congratulations, or a simple note.
- **Conduct Satisfaction Surveys**: Regularly gather client feedback through surveys or informal conversations. Use this feedback to improve your services.
- **Stay Informed and Educated**: Keep up-to-date with the latest in fitness training and health education to provide the best possible advice and support to your clients.

PROVIDING exceptional client service in the fitness industry is about creating personalized experiences, building strong relationships, and continually striving for excellence in your services. By following these actionable steps, you can ensure your clients not only achieve their fitness goals but also feel valued and supported throughout their journey. Remember, in the world of fitness, the strength of your client relationships is just as important as the workouts you design.

Client Engagement and Communication

How OFTEN DO we hear about the vital role of communication in any relationship, and yet find it so challenging to effectively implement, especially in a professional setting like fitness coaching? Effective communication is the cornerstone of client engagement, and utilizing technology for ongoing communication can significantly enhance this process. This section of the chapter dives into practical strategies for harnessing these tools to deepen client relationships and improve engagement.

Effective Communication Techniques for Client Engagement

- **Active Listening**: This goes beyond just hearing what clients say. It involves understanding their concerns, motivations, and aspirations. For instance, when a client talks about struggling to lose weight, it's not just about the diet or exercise plan; it's about understanding their lifestyle, habits, and emotional triggers.
- **Empathetic Responses**: Showing empathy can significantly strengthen the coach-client relationship. Acknowledge their feelings and challenges, and offer solutions that align with their emotional state.
- **Regular Updates and Check-ins**: Keep clients informed about their progress and what they can expect in their upcoming sessions. This can be as simple as a weekly text or email summarizing their achievements and goals for the next week.

Utilizing Technology for Ongoing Communication

- **Fitness Apps**: Leverage apps that allow clients to track their progress, set goals, and share these updates with you. This not only keeps them engaged but also provides you with valuable data to tailor their fitness plans.

- **Social Media Platforms**: Use platforms like Instagram or Facebook to create a community around your fitness brand. Regular posts about different workouts, nutrition tips, and motivational stories can keep clients engaged and motivated.
- **Email Newsletters**: Send out regular newsletters with fitness tips, success stories, and updates about your services. This keeps clients informed and connected to your brand.

Actionable Steps for Enhancing Client Communication

- **Implement a Client Relationship Management System (CRM)**: Use a CRM to keep track of all client interactions, preferences, and progress.
- **Set Up Automated Reminders**: Use technology to send automated workout reminders, appointment confirmations, and motivational messages.
- **Create Personalized Communication Plans**: Based on the client's preference, decide on the mode (text, email, phone calls) and frequency of communication.
- **Engage on Social Media**: Regularly post engaging content and respond to comments and messages on your social media platforms.
- **Offer Virtual Consultations**: Utilize video calling platforms for client consultations, especially for those who cannot meet in person.
- **Use Fitness Tracking Apps**: Encourage clients to use fitness apps and share their data with you for personalized feedback.
- **Conduct Regular Surveys**: Use online surveys to gather feedback about your services and communication methods.

IN CONCLUSION, client engagement and communication in the fitness industry are about creating a two-way street where clients feel heard, valued, and motivated. By effectively leveraging technology and personalizing your communication approach, you can build stronger, more meaningful relationships with your clients. Remember, in the world of fitness coaching, your ability to connect with your clients can be just as important as your expertise in fitness training.

Program Adaptation and Progress Tracking

"ADAPTATION IS THE KEY TO SURVIVAL," a principle that resonates profoundly in the realm of fitness coaching. As client needs and goals evolve, so must the programs designed to meet them. Equally critical is tracking progress, which not only measures growth but also fuels client satisfaction and motivation. This section delves into the nuances of program adaptation and the effective implementation of progress tracking, providing readers with actionable insights for fostering client success.

Adapting Programs to Evolving Client Needs and Goals

- Understanding Client Evolution: Clients' goals can shift due to various factors like lifestyle changes, age, or even shifting interests. For instance, a client initially focused on weight loss might shift their focus to strength training or flexibility.
- Flexible Program Design: Programs must be malleable. This includes having a variety of workout routines and being able to adjust the intensity, duration, and type of exercises based on the client's current status and feedback.
- Continual Assessment: Regularly assess the client's progress and satisfaction with the program. This could be done through bi-weekly or monthly check-ins. For example, if a client reports plateauing, it may be time to intensify or alter their workout regimen.

. . .

Implementing Progress Tracking for Client Satisfaction

- Establishing Clear Metrics: Define clear, measurable goals and milestones. This could range from weight targets and muscle gain to endurance levels or flexibility improvements.
- Utilizing Technology: Leverage digital tools like fitness trackers and apps that monitor progress in real-time. This not only provides tangible data but also a visual representation of progress that can be highly motivating.
- Celebrating Milestones: Acknowledge and celebrate when clients reach their milestones. This could be as simple as a congratulatory message or highlighting their achievements on your social media platforms.

Actionable Steps for Effective Program Adaptation and Progress Tracking

- **Conduct Regular Fitness Assessments**: Periodically reassess clients' fitness levels to ensure their current program aligns with their evolving goals and capabilities.
- **Personalize Communication**: Regularly discuss with clients their feelings about the program, any difficulties they are facing, and changes they desire.
- **Implement a Feedback Loop**: Create a system where clients can easily provide feedback on their training sessions, which can be used to adapt their program.
- **Leverage Fitness Apps for Tracking**: Integrate apps that monitor workout routines, dietary habits, and other relevant health metrics, ensuring clients can track their progress.

- **Educate Clients**: Help clients understand the significance of each exercise and how it contributes to their overall goals.
- **Document Progress**: Maintain a record of clients' progress, which can be reviewed together to discuss achievements and areas for improvement.
- **Be Adaptive and Flexible**: Be ready to modify training programs based on client feedback, performance, and changing goals.

THE ABILITY TO adapt fitness programs to meet the evolving needs of clients, coupled with effective progress tracking, is crucial for client satisfaction and long-term success. By embracing these practices, fitness professionals can not only enhance their clients' experiences but also build a reputation for being attentive and responsive to individual needs. Remember, in the dynamic world of fitness coaching, flexibility and attentiveness to change are your greatest allies.

Building a Community Around Your Brand

"COMMUNITY IS NOT JUST about being part of something; it's about doing something together that makes belonging matter." This quote encapsulates the essence of building a community around your brand. Fostering a sense of community among clients is not just about creating a group; it's about nurturing an environment where every member feels valued, heard, and connected. This final section explores the significance of community in enhancing client loyalty and driving referrals, offering tactical information and actionable steps to achieve this.

Fostering a Sense of Community Among Clients

- Personalized Attention: Recognize and celebrate individual achievements within the community. This can be as simple as acknowledging a client's progress in a group session or sharing success stories on social media.

- Community Events: Organize events that bring clients together, such as workshops, group challenges, or social gatherings. These events should be fun, inclusive, and reflective of the community's values.
- Engage and Listen: Encourage open communication within the community. This could be through social media groups, forums, or regular feedback sessions. Listening to clients' needs and opinions fosters a sense of belonging and respect.

Leveraging Community for Client Loyalty and Referrals

- Word of Mouth: A strong community naturally leads to word-of-mouth referrals. Clients who feel part of a supportive group are more likely to recommend your services to others.
- Loyalty Programs: Implement loyalty programs that reward clients for referrals and continued patronage. This not only encourages referrals but also acknowledges clients' contributions to the community.
- Showcase Community Success: Share stories and testimonials from community members. Highlighting these success stories not only motivates existing members but also attracts potential clients.

Actionable Steps for Building a Community Around Your Brand

- **Create a Welcoming Atmosphere**: Ensure that every interaction with clients, whether online or in person, is warm and welcoming.

- **Regular Communication**: Use newsletters, social media, or other platforms to keep clients informed and engaged with the community's activities and achievements.
- **Feedback and Adaptation**: Regularly seek feedback from community members and be willing to adapt based on their suggestions to ensure the community meets their needs.
- **Host Regular Events**: Plan and execute regular events that cater to the interests and needs of the community.
- **Recognize Individual Contributions**: Acknowledge and celebrate individual achievements and milestones within the community.
- **Encourage Peer-to-Peer Interaction**: Create opportunities for clients to interact, support, and learn from each other.
- **Showcase Real Stories**: Share real-life stories of community members, their challenges, and how they overcame them with the support of the community.

BUILDING a community around your brand is a powerful strategy to enhance client loyalty and generate referrals. It's about creating a space where clients feel a sense of belonging and mutual support. By focusing on these actionable steps and fostering a strong sense of community, you can create a loyal client base that not only believes in your brand but also advocates for it. Remember, a strong community reflects a strong brand, and its impact can extend far beyond business metrics to create meaningful and lasting relationships.

Part 3: Expanding Your Client Base

Exploring New Markets

IN A WORLD where borders are blurring, tapping into new markets has become a crucial strategy for business expansion and sustainability. The concept of exploring new client markets is not just about geographic expansion; it's about understanding and adapting to diverse customer needs and preferences, leveraging the power of globalization. This section delves into practical strategies for expanding your client base beyond your immediate locality, providing insightful, actionable steps for businesses looking to broaden their horizons.

Identifying New Client Markets

- **Market Research is Key**: Understand the demographics, cultural nuances, and consumer behavior of potential new markets. Utilize surveys, focus groups, and market analysis tools to gather data.
- **Look for Market Gaps**: Identify unmet needs or underserved areas in these new markets. This could involve offering a unique product or service that fills a void in the market.
- **Leverage Digital Platforms**: Use digital tools and social media analytics to understand the preferences of potential clients in different regions.

Strategies for Expanding Your Client Base Beyond Your Immediate Locality

- **Embrace Digital Marketing**: Develop a robust online presence that appeals to a global audience.

Tailor your website and social media content to resonate with diverse cultural groups.

- **Local Partnerships**: Collaborate with local businesses or influencers in the new markets to gain credibility and insight. This helps in understanding local market dynamics and building trust with potential clients.
- **Customization is Crucial**: Customize your offerings to suit the specific needs of each market. This might involve tweaking your product or service to align with local tastes, preferences, or regulations.
- **Consistent Branding, Diverse Approach**: Maintain core brand values, but adapt your marketing strategies to fit different cultural contexts. This includes language translations, culturally relevant advertising, and respecting local customs.

Actionable Steps for Market Expansion

- **Conduct In-depth Market Research**: Gather as much information as possible about the new market, including consumer behavior, competition, and legal requirements.
- **Develop a Localization Strategy**: Adapt your product, marketing, and customer service to align with local preferences.
- **Build a Local Network**: Establish relationships with local businesses, distributors, and influencers to understand market nuances and gain trust.
- **Invest in Digital Infrastructure**: Ensure that your online platforms can support different languages and cultural nuances.
- **Test and Learn**: Start with small-scale launches or pilot programs to test the market's response to your offerings.

- **Gather Feedback and Iterate**: Continuously collect customer feedback and be willing to make adjustments based on what you learn.
- **Monitor Performance and Scale Gradually**: Keep track of your progress and scale your operations in the new market as you gain more confidence and understanding.

In summary, exploring new markets requires a blend of strategic planning, cultural understanding, and adaptability. By conducting thorough market research, customizing offerings, and leveraging digital tools, businesses can successfully expand their client base beyond their immediate locality. Remember, the key to successful market expansion lies in understanding and respecting the diversity of consumer needs and preferences. As you embark on this journey, be open to learning, adapting, and evolving to meet the dynamic needs of the global market. This approach not only broadens your client base but also enriches your business with diverse perspectives and opportunities for growth.

Collaborations and Partnerships

Why do some fitness businesses thrive while others struggle to stay afloat? Often, the answer lies in their ability to form meaningful collaborations and partnerships. This section of the chapter delves into the art of forging alliances with other fitness professionals and businesses. It's not just about expanding your client base; it's about creating a network that benefits all parties involved, ultimately leading to mutual growth.

The Power of Collaborations in the Fitness Industry

- **Shared Expertise**: Collaborating with other fitness professionals can lead to a pooling of expertise, which can be a significant draw for clients. For instance, a yoga instructor might partner with a nutritionist to offer a holistic wellness program.

- **Joint Marketing Efforts**: Collaborations often lead to shared marketing responsibilities, broadening your reach. Joint workshops, webinars, and fitness events can attract a wider audience than solo endeavors.

Building Strategic Partnerships

- **Identify Complementary Businesses**: Look for businesses that complement rather than compete with your offerings. This could include fitness apparel stores, health food cafes, or physiotherapy clinics.
- **Align on Values and Goals**: Ensure that the businesses you partner with share similar values and goals. This alignment is crucial for a long-lasting and fruitful partnership.
- **Create Win-Win Situations**: A successful partnership should benefit both parties. This might involve sharing client bases, resources, or expertise.

Actionable Steps for Leveraging Partnerships

- **Research Potential Partners**: Look into their business models, clientele, and reputation. Ensure they align with your brand's ethos and objectives.
- **Plan Collaborative Events**: Organize events that showcase the strengths of both partners. This could include open days, fitness challenges, or health and wellness fairs.
- **Develop Referral Programs**: Create systems where you and your partner can refer clients to each other, ensuring a mutual flow of business.

- **Utilize Social Media and Online Platforms**: Cross-promote each other's services on social media and other online platforms to maximize exposure.
- **Regularly Review and Adapt the Partnership**: Keep the lines of communication open and regularly review the partnership's effectiveness. Be open to making changes for continual improvement.
- **Measure Success**: Use key performance indicators (KPIs) to measure the success of the partnership. This could be in terms of client feedback, increased clientele, or revenue growth.
- **Network Within the Industry**: Attend industry events, workshops, and seminars to network with potential partners. Building relationships is key to identifying collaboration opportunities.

COLLABORATIONS AND PARTNERSHIPS in the fitness industry are not just about expanding client bases; they are about enhancing the overall value offered to clients. By combining resources, expertise, and marketing efforts, fitness professionals can create a synergistic effect that benefits all involved parties. Remember, the most successful partnerships are those built on mutual respect, shared goals, and a genuine desire to provide the best possible service to clients. By strategically leveraging these alliances, your business can experience growth, innovation, and a stronger presence in the fitness industry.

Hosting Events and Workshops

IMAGINE A FITNESS BRAND, not just known for its exceptional training but also for its vibrant community events. This is the reality for many successful fitness enterprises. This section of the chapter delves into the strategic planning and execution of events and workshops, which are instrumental in enhancing brand exposure and fostering deep client engagement.

Strategies for Organizing Impactful Events and Workshops

- **Identify Your Audience**: Understanding your target audience is crucial. Tailor your events to meet their interests and fitness levels. This could range from beginner yoga classes to advanced strength training workshops.
- **Unique and Engaging Content**: Your events should offer something unique that cannot be found in regular sessions. This could include guest speakers, specialized training techniques, or wellness seminars.

Maximizing Client Engagement and Acquisition Through Events

- **Interactive Sessions**: Incorporate interactive elements such as Q&A sessions, live demonstrations, or group activities. This engagement is key to making the event memorable and encouraging community building.
- **Leveraging Social Media**: Utilize social media platforms for event promotion and live updates. Encourage attendees to share their experiences and tag your brand, amplifying your reach.

Actionable Steps for Successful Event Planning

- **Choose the Right Theme**: Select a theme that resonates with your brand and audience. This could be related to fitness trends, wellness, or community building.
- **Venue Selection**: The venue should align with your event's theme and be accessible to your target

audience. Consider factors like space, equipment, and ambiance.

- **Effective Marketing**: Develop a marketing strategy that includes social media promotion, email marketing, and local community outreach.
- **Collaborate with Influencers**: Partnering with fitness influencers or local celebrities can dramatically increase your event's visibility and attractiveness.
- **Post-Event Engagement**: Follow up with attendees through emails or social media. Gather feedback and share highlights to maintain the connection.
- **Analyze and Adapt**: After the event, analyze its success based on attendance, engagement, and feedback. Use these insights to improve future events.

Leveraging Events for Long-term Benefits

- **Community Building**: Successful events foster a sense of community among attendees, which can lead to increased client loyalty and word-of-mouth referrals.
- **Brand Positioning**: Regular, high-quality events position your brand as an industry leader, adding to its credibility and appeal.

HOSTING events and workshops is a dynamic way to engage existing clients and attract new ones. It's about creating an experience that resonates beyond the walls of your fitness center. By strategically planning and executing these events, you can elevate your brand, forge a strong community, and witness a significant impact on client acquisition and retention. Remember, the success of these events lies in the details – from the initial concept to post-event engagement. Keep your audience's interests at heart, and you'll create not just events, but memorable experiences that help your brand thrive in the competitive fitness industry.

Diversifying Your Offerings

IN THE REALM OF FITNESS, diversifying your offerings is akin to planting a garden with a variety of seeds, each promising to sprout into a unique and thriving plant. This concluding section of our chapter embraces the delicate balance between introducing new services and maintaining a strong core specialization, a strategy that can significantly enhance your brand's appeal and reach a broader client base.

Integrating New Services: A Strategic Approach

- **Understand Your Client Base**: Before diversifying, conduct thorough research to understand your clients' needs and preferences. This ensures that any new service you introduce aligns with their interests and enhances their overall experience.
- **Balanced Diversification**: The key is not to overextend your offerings but to integrate new services that complement your core specialization. For instance, if your fitness center specializes in weight training, consider introducing nutrition counseling or flexibility workshops.

Maintaining Specialization While Diversifying

- **Quality Over Quantity**: While it's tempting to offer a wide range of services, focus on maintaining high-quality standards in both your core area and any new offerings. This approach builds trust and credibility among your clientele.

- **Client-Centric Development**: Involve your clients in the development of new services. Gather feedback through surveys or focus groups to ensure the new offerings resonate with their needs and preferences.

Actionable Steps for Successful Diversification

- **Market Analysis**: Conduct a detailed analysis of market trends and competitor offerings to identify potential areas for diversification.
- **Pilot Programs**: Test new services through short-term pilot programs. This minimizes risk and allows for adjustments based on client feedback.
- **Training and Development**: Ensure your staff is adequately trained and equipped to deliver the new services with the same level of expertise and professionalism as your core offerings.
- **Marketing and Promotion**: Utilize a targeted marketing strategy to promote your new services, highlighting how they complement and enhance your existing offerings.
- **Continuous Evaluation**: Regularly assess the performance of your new services. This includes tracking client engagement, satisfaction, and financial metrics to determine their impact and success.

Leveraging Diversification for Growth

- **Client Retention and Attraction**: By offering a range of services, you not only retain current clients by meeting their evolving needs but also attract new clients seeking a holistic fitness experience.
- **Brand Differentiation**: Diversified services set your brand apart in a competitive market, positioning

you as a comprehensive solution for fitness and wellness needs.

DIVERSIFYING your offerings is a strategic move that, when executed thoughtfully, can significantly enhance your brand's value and appeal. It's about understanding your clients, maintaining a high standard of quality, and continually evaluating the impact of these new services. By doing so, you can expand your client base while staying true to your core mission and values. Remember, successful diversification is not just about adding services; it's about enriching the client experience and growing your brand in a sustainable and impactful way. As you embark on this journey of diversification, keep your clients' needs at the forefront, and let their feedback guide your path to innovation and growth.

Techniques and Process

Part 1: Attracting Clients

IDENTIFYING Your Ideal Client

- Defining the characteristics of your target client.
- Tailoring your marketing to appeal to your ideal client.

Effective Advertising Techniques

- Exploring various advertising methods for maximum impact.
- Utilizing both online and offline advertising for client acquisition.

Leveraging Social Proof

- Harnessing the power of social proof in attracting clients.
- Implementing client reviews and endorsements in your marketing.

Offering Promotions and Discounts

- Creating enticing offers to attract new clients.
- Balancing promotions with profitability.

Part 2: Client Retention Strategies

Providing Exceptional Client Service

- Delivering personalized attention and exceptional service.
- Building strong, lasting relationships with clients.

Client Engagement and Communication

- Effective communication techniques for client engagement.
- Utilizing technology for ongoing client communication.

Program Adaptation and Progress Tracking

- Adapting programs to evolving client needs and goals.
- Implementing progress tracking for client satisfaction.

Building a Community Around Your Brand

- Fostering a sense of community among clients.
- Leveraging community to enhance client loyalty and referrals.

Part 3: Expanding Your Client Base

Exploring New Markets

- Identifying and tapping into new client markets.
- Strategies for expanding your client base beyond your immediate locality.

Collaborations and Partnerships

- Forming collaborations with other fitness professionals and businesses.
- Leveraging partnerships for mutual growth and client base expansion.

Hosting Events and Workshops

- Organizing events and workshops for brand exposure.
- Using events as a platform for client engagement and acquisition.

Diversifying Your Offerings

- Introducing new services or programs to attract diverse clients.
- Balancing specialization with diversification in your offerings.

Identifying Your Ideal Client:

- **Real-World Scenario**: Just like Sarah, who transformed her gym by focusing on working professionals, you can redefine your fitness business by identifying a specific demographic. This might involve targeting young mothers, busy professionals, or retirees.
- **Application**: Conduct surveys, analyze client data, and observe trends to pinpoint your ideal client. Tailor your services, marketing, and ambiance to suit their preferences.

Effective Advertising Techniques:

- **Real-World Scenario**: A gym successfully combines online ads targeting local professionals with community events to broaden its reach.
- **Application**: Use social media for targeted ads and SEO for online visibility. Offline, participate in community events and collaborate with local businesses for cross-promotion.

Leveraging Social Proof:

- **Real-World Scenario**: A fitness center showcases video testimonials of clients' transformation stories on its website and social media.
- **Application**: Encourage clients to share their experiences, manage online reviews actively, and use clients' success stories in your marketing materials.

Offering Promotions and Discounts:

- **Real-World Scenario**: A yoga studio offers a first-class free promotion, attracting new clients without significantly impacting profitability.
- **Application**: Design promotions that align with your clients' desires but also consider long-term business sustainability.

Action Item Checklist:

ATTRACTING CLIENTS:

- **Define Your Target Market**: Identify key characteristics like age, profession, fitness goals.
- **Develop Tailored Marketing Strategies**: Create campaigns specifically designed for your target audience.
- **Implement Social Proof Tactics**: Encourage clients to leave reviews and share their stories.
- **Design Sustainable Promotions**: Offer deals that attract new clients while maintaining profitability.

CLIENT RETENTION:

- **Personalize Client Experience**: Regularly update client profiles and tailor services to individual needs.
- **Enhance Communication**: Schedule regular check-ins and updates with clients.
- **Organize Community Events**: Plan activities that foster client interaction and community building.
- **Recognize Client Achievements**: Celebrate milestones and provide recognition.

EXPANDING CLIENT BASE:

- **Conduct Market Research for Expansion**: Use surveys and analysis tools to understand new markets.
- **Develop Localization Strategies**: Adapt your offerings to fit different cultural contexts.
- **Network and Build Partnerships**: Establish connections with local businesses and influencers.
- **Plan and Execute Collaborative Events**: Organize events that showcase collaborative efforts.

Resource List:

TOOLS:

- **Hootsuite or Buffer for Social Media Management**: Streamlines your online advertising efforts.
- **Google Analytics**: Offers insights into your website's performance and audience demographics.
- **SurveyMonkey**: For conducting market research and client feedback surveys.

BOOKS AND READING MATERIAL:

- "Contagious: How to Build Word of Mouth in the Digital Age" by Jonah Berger: Explores the power of word-of-mouth marketing.
- "Influence: The Psychology of Persuasion" by Robert Cialdini: Provides insights into client behavior and decision-making.

ADDITIONAL RESOURCES:

- **Online Courses**: Look for courses on digital marketing and client relationship management.
- **Fitness Business Forums**: Platforms like thebodybuilding.com forums offer community advice and support.

mastering the art of personal trainer entrepreneurship

. . .

IN THE BUSTLING world of fitness, the role of a personal trainer is often likened to a beacon, guiding individuals toward their health and fitness goals. Yet, beyond this pivotal role lies a less explored, but equally thrilling path: entrepreneurship in personal training. Chapter 4 unfolds the vibrant tapestry of opportunities and strategies that await personal trainers eager to embrace entrepreneurship, transforming their passion for fitness into a flourishing business.

IMAGINE TAKING the reins of your career, steering it towards uncharted territories of success and fulfillment. This chapter is the compass for such a journey, guiding fitness professionals through the intricacies of establishing and nurturing a thriving business in the fitness industry. It's not just about being a great trainer; it's about becoming a savvy entrepreneur who can navigate the business landscape with confidence and creativity.

EMBARKING on this path requires more than just expertise in fitness; it demands an entrepreneurial mindset, a keen understanding of the market, and the ability to adapt and grow in an ever-changing industry. It's about spotting opportunities, building meaningful relationships, and continuously evolving to meet the needs of a diverse clientele. From crafting a unique brand identity to leveraging the latest digital marketing strategies, this chapter is a deep dive into the essential skills and knowledge needed to excel as a fitness entrepreneur.

CRUCIALLY, the journey of a fitness entrepreneur is as much about personal growth as it is about business success. It's an opportunity to challenge oneself, to step out of the comfort zone, and to make a lasting impact on the lives of others. With each section of this chapter, readers will gain valuable insights into the art of balancing client satisfaction with business acumen, ensuring their venture not only survives but thrives in the competitive world of fitness.

LET this chapter be your guide to mastering the art of personal trainer entrepreneurship, where every step forward is a step towards realizing your potential as both a fitness expert and a business visionary. Prepare to embark on an enlightening journey that promises to reshape your perspective on what it means to be a personal trainer in today's dynamic world.

Part 1: Entrepreneurial Mindset and Skills

Developing an Entrepreneurial Mindset

IN THE HEART of a bustling city, there was once a small gym whose transformation story epitomizes the essence of an entrepreneurial mindset. The gym's owner, Jake, a former athlete turned personal trainer, found himself grappling with the challenges of transforming his passion into a profitable venture. His journey wasn't just about fitness; it was a lesson in resilience, adaptability, and entrepreneurial spirit.

JAKE'S STORY begins with his dream of creating a space that went beyond traditional fitness training. He envisioned a place where personal growth and physical training went hand in hand. However, like many entrepreneurs, he faced hurdles. Membership numbers were not growing as anticipated, and financial pressures were mounting. It was a critical point where many would consider giving up, but Jake saw it as an opportunity to pivot and grow.

THE ENTREPRENEURIAL MINDSET is not just about great ideas; it's about the resilience to face setbacks and the flexibility to adapt strategies. For Jake, this meant re-evaluating his business model and client engagement strategies. He began by deeply understanding his target audience, which were working professionals seeking more than just physical fitness. They wanted a space where they could destress, connect, and find balance in their hectic lives.

ARMED WITH THIS INSIGHT, Jake revamped his gym's approach. He introduced wellness workshops, mindfulness sessions, and community-building events, transforming his gym into a holistic wellness hub. This shift was a bold move, requiring not just financial investment but also a leap of faith in his vision.

THIS TRANSFORMATION WASN'T IMMEDIATE. It involved trial and error, listening to client feedback, and continuously refining the offerings. What made Jake successful was his ability to stay focused on his vision while being agile enough to make necessary changes. He cultivated a mindset that viewed challenges as stepping stones rather than obstacles.

Cultivating the Entrepreneurial Mindset

TO DEVELOP AN ENTREPRENEURIAL MINDSET, start by embracing adaptability. Be prepared to change course when necessary and view failures as opportunities to learn and grow. It's about staying committed to your vision while being flexible in your approach.

HERE ARE key steps to nurture this mindset:

- **Embrace Continuous Learning:** Always look for ways to enhance your knowledge and skills. This could mean attending workshops, seeking mentorship, or staying updated with industry trends.
- **Develop Resilience:** Resilience is the backbone of entrepreneurship. It's about having the mental toughness to face setbacks and keep moving forward.
- **Foster Creativity and Innovation:** Encourage yourself to think outside the box. Innovation is key to differentiating your business in a competitive market.
- **Build Strong Networks:** Relationships are crucial in business. Network with other professionals in your industry to learn, share experiences, and find support.
- **Stay Client-Focused:** Always keep the needs and feedback of your clients at the forefront. Their satisfaction is the ultimate barometer of your success.

- **Practice Financial Prudence:** Manage your resources wisely. Understand your business finances and plan for sustainability.

Overcoming Challenges with Resilience

RESILIENCE IN ENTREPRENEURSHIP is not just about bouncing back from challenges; it's about using those challenges to propel your business forward. Here are actionable steps to build resilience:

- **Maintain a Positive Outlook:** Train your mind to see the positive in every situation. A positive attitude is infectious and can keep you and your team motivated.
- **Set Realistic Goals:** Having clear, achievable goals can help you stay focused, especially during tough times.
- **Build a Supportive Network:** Surround yourself with people who believe in your vision and can offer practical advice and emotional support.
- **Take Care of Your Well-being:** Your health and well-being are crucial. Regular exercise, a balanced diet, and sufficient rest are vital to maintain the energy and focus needed for your business.
- **Reflect and Learn from Setbacks:** Analyze what went wrong and use these insights to improve your strategies and decisions.
- **Stay Flexible:** Be willing to adapt your business model, strategies, or products/services in response to changing market needs or challenges.

DEVELOPING an entrepreneurial mindset and overcoming challenges with resilience are crucial for success in the ever-evolving world of fitness entrepreneurship. It's about the harmony between staying true to your vision and adapting to the realities of the business world. As you navigate through your entrepreneurial journey, remember that every challenge is an opportunity to grow stronger and every setback a chance to come back more robust. Embrace this mindset, and you will be well on your way to building a successful and resilient fitness business.

Essential Business Skills for Trainers

DID you know that most personal trainers enter the industry fueled by their passion for fitness but often find themselves unprepared for the business side of their profession? This gap in business acumen can be the line between thriving and merely surviving in the fitness industry. As a personal trainer, developing your entrepreneurial skills is just as important as perfecting your squat technique.

Acquiring Business Skills Critical for Fitness Entrepreneurs

ONE OF THE first skills to master is financial management. It's not just about setting prices for your services; it's understanding cash flow, managing expenses, and planning for financial growth. Start by setting up a simple accounting system to track your income and expenses. Tools like QuickBooks or FreshBooks are user-friendly and designed for small business owners.

NEXT, delve into marketing. In today's digital world, a strong online presence is essential. This includes creating a professional website, being active on social media platforms where your potential clients are, and understanding the basics of digital marketing. These tools are not just about promoting your services; they're about building your brand and connecting with your community.

· · ·

NETWORKING IS ANOTHER VITAL SKILL. Building relationships with other fitness professionals, local businesses, and community members can lead to new opportunities and referrals. Attend local events, join professional groups, and don't hesitate to collaborate with others.

LASTLY, customer service excellence is crucial. This means not only delivering top-notch training sessions but also creating a memorable experience for your clients. Responding promptly to inquiries, remembering personal details about your clients, and consistently showing your appreciation can turn a one-time client into a loyal advocate for your business.

Balancing Fitness Expertise with Business Acumen

THE KEY to balancing fitness expertise with business acumen is integration. Your business skills should complement your training skills, not compete with them. For instance, use your understanding of fitness to create targeted marketing campaigns that speak directly to your clients' needs.

DEVELOP a system that allows you to manage your time effectively between training clients and managing your business. Set aside specific times for administrative tasks, marketing efforts, and professional development. Utilize technology to streamline these processes – scheduling apps, automated email responses, and digital marketing tools can save you time and effort.

REGULARLY ASSESS YOUR BUSINESS PERFORMANCE. Just like you track a client's progress, track your business growth. Set measurable goals for different aspects of your business and review them periodically. This practice will help you identify what's working and what needs improvement.

Actionable Steps for Fitness Entrepreneurs

- **Set Up a Basic Accounting System:** Choose user-friendly software to manage your finances. Regularly track your income and expenses.
- **Develop a Strong Online Presence:** Build a professional website and maintain active social media profiles. Engage with your audience through quality content.
- **Learn Digital Marketing Basics:** Understand the fundamentals of SEO, content marketing, and social media advertising.
- **Engage in Networking:** Attend local fitness events, join professional groups, and build relationships within the fitness community.
- **Prioritize Customer Service:** Develop a client-centric approach. Be responsive, personable, and appreciative of your clients.
- **Utilize Technology:** Incorporate apps and software to streamline scheduling, communication, and marketing.
- **Regular Business Assessments:** Set business goals and regularly review your progress. Adjust strategies as needed.
- **Financial Planning:** Plan for the future of your business. Set financial goals and strategies for growth.

THE PATH to becoming a successful fitness entrepreneur involves more than just fitness knowledge. It requires a blend of business savvy, continual learning, and the ability to adapt to the ever-changing landscape of the fitness industry. By honing these essential business skills and integrating them with your fitness expertise, you can create a sustainable and thriving business. Remember, your growth as a fitness entrepreneur is a journey, not a destination. Embrace each challenge as an opportunity to learn and grow, and you'll find success both in and out of the gym.

. . .

Time Management and Productivity

"TIME IS the coin of your life. It is the only coin you have, and only you can determine how it will be spent," said Carl Sandburg. This profound truth strikes at the heart of every entrepreneur, especially in the fitness industry, where balancing client sessions, business management, and personal commitments can feel like a constant juggling act. The essence of effective time management lies not in doing more in less time but in doing the right things at the right time.

Effective Time Management Strategies for Busy Entrepreneurs

SUCCESSFUL ENTREPRENEURS UNDERSTAND that time management is about prioritization. The first step is to identify your high-value activities – tasks that directly contribute to your business growth and client satisfaction. These might include developing new training programs, networking, or enhancing your professional skills.

ONE EFFECTIVE METHOD is the Eisenhower Matrix, which categorizes tasks into four quadrants based on their urgency and importance. This tool helps you focus on tasks that are important but not urgent, which are often the ones that drive long-term success.

ANOTHER KEY STRATEGY is setting clear boundaries. This could mean having specific work hours, limiting time spent on emails, or saying no to tasks that do not align with your business goals. Time blocking is a practical approach here, where you allocate specific time slots for different activities throughout your day.

. . .

DELEGATION IS another critical aspect of time management. Identify tasks that can be outsourced or assigned to others, freeing up your time to focus on core business activities. This might include administrative work, marketing efforts, or even certain aspects of client management.

Tools and Techniques for Maximizing Productivity

IN TODAY'S DIGITAL AGE, numerous tools can help streamline your processes and boost productivity. Project management tools like Trello or Asana are excellent for organizing tasks, setting deadlines, and tracking progress. They provide a visual overview of your projects and can be shared with team members or collaborators.

FOR TIME TRACKING, tools like Toggle or Harvest can help you understand how much time you're spending on various tasks. This insight is invaluable for identifying time-wasting activities and making more informed decisions about how to allocate your time.

AUTOMATING routine tasks can save a significant amount of time. Whether it's scheduling social media posts using tools like Buffer or automating appointment bookings with Calendly, automation frees you up to focus on more strategic tasks.

FINALLY, don't underestimate the power of a well-organized physical and digital workspace. A clutter-free environment can significantly enhance focus and efficiency. Digital organization, such as a well-structured file system and a clean email inbox, also plays a crucial role in productivity.

Actionable Steps for Fitness Entrepreneurs

- **Identify High-Value Activities:** List down tasks that have the most significant impact on your business and prioritize them.
- **Implement the Eisenhower Matrix:** Categorize your tasks into urgent/important, important/not urgent, urgent/not important, and neither urgent nor important.
- **Set Clear Boundaries:** Define your work hours and stick to them. Learn to say no to distractions and tasks that don't align with your goals.
- **Time Blocking:** Allocate specific time slots for different activities and stick to this schedule as closely as possible.
- **Delegate:** Identify tasks that can be outsourced or assigned to others and take steps to delegate them effectively.
- **Use Project Management Tools:** Implement tools like Trello or Asana for organizing tasks and managing projects.
- **Track Your Time:** Use time tracking tools to analyze how you spend your time and identify areas for improvement.
- **Automate Routine Tasks:** Identify tasks that can be automated and implement tools to do so.
- **Organize Your Workspace:** Keep your physical and digital workspace organized to enhance focus and efficiency.
- **Regular Reviews:** Periodically review your time management strategies and adjust as needed.

MASTERING time management and productivity is a continual process of learning, adjusting, and evolving. By implementing these strategies and tools, fitness entrepreneurs can not only enhance their efficiency but also find more balance and fulfillment in their professional and personal lives. Remember, the goal is not to fill every minute with work, but to use your time in a way that aligns with your personal and professional goals, ultimately leading to greater success and satisfaction.

Continuous Learning and Development

"EDUCATION IS NOT the filling of a pot but the lighting of a fire." This quote by W.B. Yeats beautifully encapsulates the essence of continuous learning and development, particularly in the dynamic realm of fitness entrepreneurship. The journey of a fitness entrepreneur is not a one-time course but a lifelong adventure of growth, adaptation, and improvement. The key to thriving in this ever-evolving industry lies not just in acquiring knowledge but in fostering a mindset of ceaseless curiosity and growth.

Embracing Continuous Learning for Personal and Business Growth

THE FITNESS INDUSTRY, like many others, is in a state of constant flux, with new research, techniques, and trends emerging regularly. Staying updated is not just a matter of professional responsibility; it's a strategic advantage. Continuous learning helps you stay ahead of the curve, ensuring your business remains relevant and competitive.

HOWEVER, embracing continuous learning goes beyond staying updated on industry trends. It's about cultivating a mindset that views every experience, challenge, and interaction as an opportunity to learn. This mindset transforms the way you approach your business, turning obstacles into learning opportunities and failures into stepping stones for growth.

Resources and Strategies for Ongoing Professional Development

SEVERAL RESOURCES ARE available for fitness entrepreneurs seeking continuous professional development. These include:

- **Industry Conferences and Workshops:** Regularly attending industry events provides invaluable insights into emerging trends and best practices. These events are also excellent networking opportunities, allowing you to learn from and collaborate with peers.
- **Online Courses and Certifications:** Platforms like Coursera, Udemy, and specialized fitness education websites offer a range of courses that can enhance your skills and knowledge.
- **Professional Reading:** Keeping up with industry-related books, journals, and articles is crucial. Publications like the Journal of Strength and Conditioning Research and books by renowned fitness experts can provide deep insights.
- **Mentorship and Coaching:** Engaging with a mentor or business coach who has navigated the path of fitness entrepreneurship can offer personalized guidance and help you avoid common pitfalls.
- **Feedback Loops:** Establishing a system for client and peer feedback can provide valuable insights into areas for improvement and new learning opportunities.

Actionable Steps for Fitness Entrepreneurs

- **Develop a Personal Learning Plan:** Identify areas where you need improvement or new skills you want to acquire. Set specific learning goals and timelines.
- **Allocate Time for Learning:** Dedicate a regular time slot in your schedule for educational activities,

whether it's attending a seminar, reading a book, or taking an online course.

- **Join Professional Groups:** Engage with professional groups and forums to stay connected with industry trends and discussions.
- **Reflect and Apply:** After learning something new, reflect on how it can be applied to your business. Implement these learnings in small, manageable steps to see what works best for your setup.
- **Seek Feedback:** Regularly seek feedback from clients and peers about your services and use this information to guide your learning priorities.
- **Embrace Change:** Be open to changing your methods and strategies based on new learnings. Flexibility is key to growth and adaptation.
- **Share Your Knowledge:** Sharing your learnings with your team or through workshops can reinforce your understanding and position you as a thought leader in your field.

CONTINUOUS LEARNING and development are not just about accumulating knowledge; they're about cultivating a mindset that embraces growth, adaptability, and resilience. As a fitness entrepreneur, your commitment to learning directly impacts your personal development and the success of your business. Remember, the quest for knowledge is endless, and each step on this path is an opportunity to ignite a brighter future for your business and yourself.

Part 2: Financial Management for Fitness Entrepreneurs

Budgeting and Financial Planning

"SHOW me the numbers and I'll tell you the story," a successful fitness entrepreneur once said. This statement hits the core of budgeting and financial planning in the fitness industry. Creating and managing a budget isn't just about tracking expenses and revenue; it's about crafting a story of your business's growth, challenges, and potential. Let's dive into the art of budgeting and financial planning to ensure the long-term sustainability of your fitness business.

Creating and Managing a Budget for Your Fitness Business

A BUDGET IS your business's financial blueprint. It guides you in making informed decisions and helps prevent unnecessary expenditures. Here's how to create and manage an effective budget:

- **Understand Your Revenue Streams:** Identify all your income sources, such as memberships, personal training sessions, and merchandise sales. Understanding where your money comes from helps you predict future income.
- **Categorize Your Expenses:** Break down your expenses into categories like rent, equipment, staff salaries, and marketing. This categorization makes it easier to track and control spending.
- **Set Financial Goals:** Determine what you want to achieve financially, whether it's increasing profit margins, expanding your facility, or investing in new equipment.

- **Monitor and Adjust Regularly:** Your budget is a living document. Regularly compare your actual income and expenses against your budget and adjust as needed.
- **Plan for Emergencies:** Set aside a contingency fund for unexpected expenses, such as equipment repairs or a sudden drop in membership.

Financial Planning for Long-Term Business Sustainability

LONG-TERM FINANCIAL PLANNING involves strategizing for the future while being adaptable to changing market conditions. Here are key strategies:

- **Forecast Future Growth:** Use your current financial data to predict future revenue and expenses. This foresight helps in making strategic business decisions.
- **Manage Cash Flow:** Ensure you have enough cash to cover day-to-day operations. Efficient cash flow management prevents financial strain on your business.
- **Invest in Growth:** Identify opportunities for business growth, such as opening new locations or offering new services, and plan your finances accordingly.
- **Prepare for Tax Obligations:** Understand your tax obligations and plan for them in advance to avoid last-minute stress and penalties.
- **Seek Professional Advice:** Consult with a financial advisor for personalized advice tailored to your business's specific needs and goals.

BUDGETING and financial planning are crucial for the sustainability and growth of your fitness business. They provide a clear financial picture, enabling you to make strategic decisions with confidence. By mastering these financial skills, you position your business not just to survive, but to thrive and expand in the competitive fitness industry. Remember, the success of your fitness business isn't just measured by the number of clients you train, but also by the robustness of your financial health.

Revenue Streams and Diversification

DID you know that most successful fitness businesses don't just rely on memberships or personal training fees? They thrive by creating multiple streams of income. This approach not only boosts revenue but also buffers the business against market fluctuations. Let's explore how you can identify and develop various revenue streams and diversify your income to mitigate business risks.

Identifying and Developing Multiple Revenue Streams

- **Diversify Your Offerings:** Beyond basic gym memberships, consider offering specialized classes, online training, nutritional counseling, or wellness workshops. Each new service is a new stream of revenue.
- **Retail and Merchandise:** Selling fitness-related products like supplements, apparel, or equipment can add a significant revenue stream. Collaborate with brands for a mutual benefit.
- **Corporate Wellness Programs:** Partner with local businesses to offer their employees special membership deals or personalized wellness programs. It's a win-win for both parties.
- **Online Content:** Develop online resources like workout videos, e-books, or a subscription-based

website. This digital approach can attract a global audience.

- **Events and Workshops:** Host fitness events, workshops, or retreats. These can be great for both community building and generating additional income.

Diversifying Income to Mitigate Business Risks

- **Understand Market Trends:** Stay informed about fitness industry trends. This knowledge helps in adapting your offerings to what's currently in demand.
- **Customer Feedback:** Regularly gather feedback from your clients. Their input can guide you in creating services or products that meet their evolving needs.
- **Flexibility in Business Model:** Be open to adjusting your business model. For instance, if you notice a surge in demand for online classes, consider enhancing your digital offerings.
- **Regular Financial Review:** Regularly analyze your income streams to understand which are most profitable and which may need revamping or discontinuation.
- **Risk Management:** Have a risk management strategy. This could include insurance, emergency funds, or backup plans in case a primary revenue stream falters.

BY DIVERSIFYING YOUR REVENUE STREAMS, you not only increase your earning potential but also make your business more resilient to market changes. Each new stream you develop or enhance should align with your business's core values and strengths. Remember, the goal is not just to increase revenue but to build a sustainable, flexible, and resilient business that can adapt and grow in the ever-changing fitness industry landscape.

Managing Expenses and Cash Flow

"REMEMBER that the goal is not to make money, it's to manage money." This simple yet profound statement sheds light on the essential aspect of running a successful fitness business – managing expenses and maintaining cash flow. Let's dive into effective strategies and tools that can help you in this vital area of financial management.

Effective Strategies for Managing Expenses

- **Budget Creation and Adherence:** Start by creating a detailed budget. This plan should include all potential expenses, from rent and utilities to marketing and staff salaries. Stick to this budget as closely as possible, making adjustments only when necessary.
- **Cost Reduction Techniques:** Regularly review your expenses and identify areas where costs can be reduced without compromising quality. Negotiating with suppliers, reducing energy consumption, and streamlining operations are all effective strategies.
- **Use of Technology:** Implement financial management software to track expenses in real-time. This technology not only saves time but also provides accurate data for better decision-making.
- **Regular Financial Reviews:** Conduct monthly financial reviews to monitor the health of your business. This allows you to spot trends, address issues promptly, and make informed decisions.

Maintaining Cash Flow

- **Diversifying Income Sources:** As discussed in the previous section, having multiple revenue streams can significantly aid in maintaining healthy cash flow.
- **Effective Billing and Collection Practices:** Implement efficient billing systems and follow up on late payments promptly. Offering multiple payment options can also improve cash flow.
- **Cash Reserve:** Build a cash reserve to cushion your business against unforeseen financial challenges. This fund can be a lifesaver during slow periods or emergencies.

Tools and Practices for Financial Tracking and Analysis

- **Accounting Software:** Use reliable accounting software to track income and expenses. This software often comes with analytical tools to help understand financial trends and patterns.
- **Professional Assistance:** Consider hiring a financial advisor or accountant. Their expertise can be invaluable in managing complex financial aspects of your business.
- **Regular Audits:** Conduct regular internal or external audits to ensure all financial transactions are recorded accurately and policies are being followed.
- **Leveraging Financial Reports:** Generate and analyze financial reports such as profit and loss statements, balance sheets, and cash flow statements. These documents provide a comprehensive view of your business's financial health.

MANAGING expenses and maintaining cash flow requires diligence, foresight, and a willingness to adapt. By employing these strategies and tools, you can ensure the financial stability and growth of your fitness business. Remember, it's not just about how much you earn, but how well you manage what you earn that determines the success of your venture.

Investing in Growth and Expansion

"INVESTING in growth is not about spending money, but about understanding where each dollar can take you." This powerful statement embodies the essence of this chapter: identifying opportunities for business investment and balancing risk and reward in growth strategies. Let's explore the tactical steps and insights for expanding your fitness business effectively.

Identifying Opportunities for Business Investment

- **Market Research:** Conduct thorough market research to identify trends and gaps in the fitness industry. This research can reveal new market segments, innovative service offerings, or technological advancements that your business can capitalize on.
- **Customer Feedback:** Regularly gather and analyze customer feedback. This information is invaluable in understanding what your clients want and how you can improve or expand your services to meet their needs.
- **Competitor Analysis:** Study your competitors closely. Understanding their strengths and weaknesses can help you identify unique opportunities for your business.
- **Networking and Industry Events:** Engage in networking and attend industry events. These platforms often provide insights into emerging trends and new business opportunities.

Balancing Risk and Reward in Business Growth Strategies

- **Risk Assessment:** Before making any significant investment, assess the potential risks involved. This includes financial risks, market risks, and operational risks.
- **Scalability:** Focus on scalable investments. Scalability means the business can handle a growing amount of work or a potential expansion in its output or client base without being hampered by its structure or available resources.
- **Financial Planning:** Ensure that you have solid financial planning. Use projections and forecasts to understand the potential financial impact of any investment.
- **Diversification:** Diversify your investments. This approach helps mitigate risks by not putting all your eggs in one basket.

Tools and Practices for Financial Tracking and Analysis

- **Financial Tracking Software:** Utilize robust financial tracking software to monitor your investments and their returns. This tool is crucial for keeping an eye on cash flow and profitability.
- **Key Performance Indicators (KPIs):** Establish and monitor KPIs specific to your investments. These metrics will help you measure success and identify areas needing improvement.
- **Regular Reviews:** Conduct regular reviews of your investment strategy. This ongoing evaluation allows you to adjust your approach in response to changing market conditions or business needs.
- **Professional Advice:** Seek professional financial advice when necessary. An expert can provide

valuable insights into complex investment decisions and tax implications.

INVESTING in growth and expansion is a crucial step in taking your fitness business to new heights. By identifying the right opportunities, balancing risks and rewards, and using effective tools for financial tracking and analysis, you can pave the way for sustainable business growth. Remember, growth is not just about expansion; it's about making strategic decisions that align with your business goals and the evolving needs of your market.

IN WRAPPING UP THIS EXPLORATION, it's vital to remember that growth is a journey that requires patience, strategic planning, and an unwavering commitment to your business vision. Embrace this journey with an open mind, and let your passion for fitness and entrepreneurship guide you towards new and exciting horizons.

Techniques and Process

Part 1: Entrepreneurial Mindset and Skills

Developing an Entrepreneurial Mindset

- Cultivating the mindset necessary for successful entrepreneurship.
- Overcoming challenges and setbacks with resilience.

Essential Business Skills for Trainers

- Acquiring business skills critical for fitness entrepreneurs.
- Balancing fitness expertise with business acumen.

Time Management and Productivity

- Effective time management strategies for busy entrepreneurs.
- Tools and techniques for maximizing productivity.

Continuous Learning and Development

- Embracing continuous learning for personal and business growth.
- Resources and strategies for ongoing professional development.

Part 2: Financial Management for Fitness Entrepreneurs

Budgeting and Financial Planning

- Creating and managing a budget for your fitness business.
- Financial planning for long-term business sustainability.

Revenue Streams and Diversification

- Identifying and developing multiple revenue streams.
- Diversifying income to mitigate business risks.

Managing Expenses and Cash Flow

- Effective strategies for managing expenses and maintaining cash flow.
- Tools and practices for financial tracking and analysis.

Investing in Growth and Expansion

- Identifying opportunities for business investment.
- Balancing risk and reward in business growth strategies.

Developing an Entrepreneurial Mindset:

- **Scenario:** Just like Jake transformed his gym, envision adapting your training services to meet evolving market demands, perhaps by incorporating virtual training sessions or specialized fitness programs.
- **Process:** Analyze client feedback, market trends, and personal passions to identify potential areas of expansion or innovation.

Financial Management Skills:

- **Scenario:** Imagine setting competitive pricing for personalized training packages while keeping track of operational costs.
- **Process:** Regularly update a budget spreadsheet, track expenses and revenues, and adjust your business strategy based on financial insights.

Effective Marketing Strategies:

- **Scenario:** Creating a strong online presence through social media engagement, targeted advertising, and content marketing.
- **Process:** Develop a marketing calendar, identify key platforms for your audience, and consistently create and share engaging, fitness-focused content.

Networking and Building Relationships:

- **Scenario:** Collaborating with local businesses for wellness programs, or connecting with other fitness professionals for joint ventures.
- **Process:** Attend community events, join fitness forums online, and actively seek collaborative opportunities.

Balancing Client Satisfaction with Business Acumen:

- **Scenario:** Offering personalized training while also managing the business aspects like scheduling and financial planning.

- **Process:** Use client management software for scheduling and feedback while dedicating specific times for business development tasks.

Action Item Checklist

Set Up a Basic Accounting System:

- Choose accounting software suitable for small businesses.
- Enter all financial transactions regularly.
- Monitor your financial status weekly.

Develop a Strong Online Presence:

- Create a professional website with details about your services.
- Set up and regularly update social media profiles.
- Engage with your audience through posts, blogs, or videos.

Initiate Networking and Collaboration:

- Identify local businesses or fitness professionals to partner with.
- Reach out with a collaboration proposal.
- Organize or participate in joint events or programs.

Implement Effective Marketing Strategies:

- Identify your unique selling proposition (USP) and target audience.
- Create a marketing plan including online and offline strategies.
- Regularly assess the effectiveness of your marketing efforts.

BALANCE TRAINING AND BUSINESS MANAGEMENT:

- Schedule specific hours for client sessions and separate hours for business tasks.
- Use tools for scheduling and feedback collection.
- Regularly review client satisfaction and business performance.

Resource List

TOOLS:

- **QuickBooks/FreshBooks:** For financial management and budget tracking.
- **Hootsuite/Buffer:** For scheduling and managing social media posts.
- **Trello/Asana:** For project management and task organization.

Books and Reading Material:

- "Building Your Fitness Empire" by Joe Fitness: Insights into fitness business growth and management.
- "Marketing for Personal Trainers" by David Leadbetter: Strategies on effectively marketing fitness services.

navigating the digital landscape for fitness coaching

. . .

IN TODAY'S fast-paced fitness world, the secret to success might just lie in your pocket or on your desk. It's your digital device, a gateway to endless opportunities in fitness coaching. This exciting chapter unveils how personal trainers, like you, can harness the power of digital tools and platforms to redefine success in fitness coaching. Think of it like having a gym that never closes, reaching clients anytime and anywhere, with just a few clicks or taps.

IMAGINE a personal trainer from a decade ago, their world was confined to the physical boundaries of a gym. Now, picture yourself, a modern fitness coach, with the ability to break those walls down. The digital age has opened up a universe where coaching transcends physical limits. This isn't just about posting workout videos online; it's about crafting a digital ecosystem that supports, engages, and motivates clients far beyond the gym's four walls.

THIS CHAPTER DOESN'T MERELY INTRODUCE you to digital tools; it guides you on how to weave them effectively into your training fabric. You'll learn not just what these tools are, but how to use them in a way that complements your unique coaching style.

From social media platforms that let you showcase your expertise and connect with a global audience to sophisticated software that streamlines your scheduling and client management, the digital world is ripe with possibilities.

BUT, adapting to this digital era requires more than just being tech-savvy. It's about understanding the changing dynamics of fitness training and client expectations. It's about being flexible, creative, and open to learning. Your clients are no longer just those who walk through the gym doors; they are anywhere and everywhere. This chapter equips you with the know-how to meet them where they are, physically and digitally.

AS WE DELVE into this chapter, remember, it's not just about keeping up with the times; it's about staying ahead. It's about transforming from a traditional trainer to a digital-age coach who leverages technology not just for convenience, but for creating a deeper, more impactful coaching experience. Whether you're a seasoned trainer or just starting, the insights here are your first steps towards mastering the digital realm of fitness coaching. Let's embark on this enlightening path together, exploring how the digital age can amplify your coaching prowess and help you build a thriving, modern fitness business.

Part 1: Digital Tools for Fitness Coaches

Leveraging Fitness and Health Apps

IN THE REALM of fitness and health, a revolution is underway, propelled by the mighty force of digital innovation. Imagine, if you will, a world where fitness coaching transcends the limits of physical presence, where personal trainers empower their clients' journeys through the tap of an app. This section of our exploration delves into the dynamic world of fitness and health apps, unraveling how these digital tools can transform the way personal trainers engage with clients and manage their programs.

PICTURE SARAH, a personal trainer whose story mirrors a digital metamorphosis. Sarah, like many in her field, initially relied on traditional methods of client management and engagement. However, the advent of fitness apps opened a new chapter in her coaching style. She discovered that these apps were not just add-ons to her training programs but powerful catalysts for deeper client engagement and streamlined program management.

SARAH'S FORAY into the world of fitness apps began with a simple step: selecting the right apps that resonated with her unique coaching style. It was a process akin to choosing the perfect pair of running shoes; it had to be the right fit. She explored various apps, each offering unique features from workout tracking and nutritional logging to client communication and schedule management. The key was to find apps that not only simplified her administrative tasks but also added value to her clients' fitness experiences.

. . .

FOR INSTANCE, Sarah adopted an app that allowed her clients to log their workouts, track their progress, and even share their triumphs on social media. This not only motivated her clients but also gave Sarah valuable insights into their progress and areas needing more attention. Another app she chose streamlined scheduling and reminders, ensuring both she and her clients were always in sync with their training sessions.

BUT HOW DID Sarah determine which apps were right for her? She focused on several critical factors: ease of use, compatibility with her training philosophy, and the ability to provide a personalized experience to her clients. She also sought feedback from her clients, understanding their preferences and comfort with technology.

LET'S delve into how you, as a fitness professional, can harness the power of these digital tools to elevate your coaching and client engagement. The journey begins with understanding your unique coaching style and the needs of your clients. Are you focused more on high-intensity workouts or mindfulness and yoga? Do your clients prefer detailed tracking of their nutrition, or are they more inclined towards simple, user-friendly interfaces for workout logging? The answers to these questions will guide you in selecting the right apps.

NEXT, consider the ease of integration of these apps into your existing workflow. A seamless transition is crucial to avoid any disruption in your training programs. Look for apps that offer features like cloud-based data storage, multi-platform accessibility, and user-friendly interfaces. These features ensure that both you and your clients can access training plans, progress reports, and communication tools easily, whether on a smartphone, tablet, or computer.

· · ·

ANOTHER VITAL ASPECT is the privacy and security of your clients' data. Opt for apps that adhere to stringent data protection standards and respect the privacy of your clients. It's essential to build trust, ensuring your clients feel confident in sharing their information on these digital platforms.

Now, let's explore actionable steps to integrate these apps into your coaching:

- **Research and Select Apps:** Start by researching apps that align with your coaching style and client needs. Look for features like workout tracking, nutrition logging, client communication, and administrative tools.
- **Test and Evaluate:** Before fully integrating an app into your coaching, test it out. Use it for a couple of weeks to understand its functionality and ease of use.
- **Train Yourself and Your Clients:** Once you have selected an app, familiarize yourself with all its features. Then, guide your clients on how to use it effectively. This might involve creating simple tutorials or having one-on-one sessions to walk them through the app.
- **Gather Feedback:** Regularly ask for feedback from your clients on the app's usability and effectiveness. This will help you make necessary adjustments and ensure the app is meeting your and your clients' needs.
- **Monitor and Adapt:** Keep an eye on how the app impacts your clients' progress and your coaching efficiency. Be open to making changes, whether it's switching to a different app or leveraging additional features of the current app.

THE DIGITAL TRANSFORMATION in fitness coaching is not just a trend; it's the future. As a personal trainer, embracing this change by leveraging fitness and health apps can significantly enhance your client engagement and program management. It's about making a strategic choice that aligns with your coaching style and adds tangible value to your clients' fitness journeys. Remember, in this digital age, your smartphone or tablet is more than just a device; it's a tool that can unlock new potentials in your coaching career.

Website Development and Management

DID YOU KNOW THAT 38% of internet users judge a business by how its website looks? In the digital age, a professional website is not just a luxury for a fitness business; it's a necessity. This section delves into creating and managing a website that not only looks great but functions effectively for your fitness venture.

LET'S start with a real-life example: Emily, a fitness coach, saw a significant increase in client engagement and business growth after revamping her website. Initially, her site was just a digital business card with contact information. However, after incorporating essential features and functionalities, her website transformed into a dynamic platform that attracted and retained clients.

CREATING a professional website begins with understanding what makes a site effective. The goal is to build a site that reflects your brand, resonates with your target audience, and provides an excellent user experience. Here are key elements to consider:

1. **User-Friendly Design:** Your website should be easy to navigate with a clean, uncluttered layout. Users should find what they are looking for within a few clicks.

2. **Responsive Design:** With more people using mobile devices to access the internet, ensure your website is mobile-friendly. This means it should look good and work well on any device, from a desktop to a smartphone.

3. **Compelling Content:** The content on your website should speak directly to your target audience. Include details about your training philosophy, services offered, and success stories. Use language that is easy to understand and avoids technical jargon.

4. **Strong Call to Actions (CTAs):** Encourage visitors to take action, whether it's signing up for a newsletter, booking a consultation, or joining a fitness program. Clear CTAs can significantly increase client engagement.

5. **SEO Optimization:** Your website should be optimized for search engines to improve its visibility. Use relevant keywords, optimize your images, and regularly update your content to rank higher in search results.

6. **Integration with Social Media:** Link your website to your social media profiles. This integration helps in promoting your content across different platforms and increases your online presence.

7. **Online Booking and Scheduling:** Incorporate an online booking system. It allows clients to schedule appointments at their convenience and can be a game-changer in managing your time and client interactions more efficiently.

8. **Blog Section:** A blog can be a powerful tool to share your expertise, offer fitness tips, and keep your website content fresh. It also helps with SEO and establishes you as an authority in your field.

Now, let's focus on the actionable steps for creating and managing your fitness website:

1. **Choose the Right Platform:** Select a website builder that suits your skill level and needs. Platforms like WordPress, Wix, or Squarespace offer various templates and customization options.
2. **Define Your Branding:** Decide on your website's color scheme, font, and overall style that aligns with your brand identity. Consistency in branding helps in building trust and recognition.
3. **Develop a Content Strategy:** Plan what content you will include on your site. This includes text, images, videos, and blog posts. Ensure the content is engaging, informative, and relevant to your audience.
4. **Implement SEO Best Practices:** Research keywords related to your fitness services and incorporate them into your website's content. Also, focus on other SEO practices like optimizing your images and improving your site's loading speed.
5. **Regularly Update Your Website:** Keep your website updated with the latest information about your services, new blog posts, or client testimonials. Regular updates keep your site relevant and engaging.
6. **Analyze and Adapt:** Use tools like Google Analytics to track your website's performance. Analyze the data to understand user behavior and make necessary adjustments to improve user experience and engagement.

In conclusion, a well-designed and managed website is crucial for the success of your fitness business in the digital age. It's not just about creating a digital presence but about building a platform that effectively communicates your brand, engages your audience, and drives business growth. Remember, your website is often the first impression potential clients have of your business, so make it count.

Using Wearable Technology

"DATA IS the new gold in the world of fitness coaching," an industry expert once remarked. This statement profoundly captures the essence of integrating wearable technology into fitness coaching. In the final part of this chapter, we delve into how wearable technology can be harnessed for personalized coaching, transforming the way trainers interact with and guide their clients. This section will explore the strategic application of data from wearables and how it can be a game-changer in the fitness industry.

Harnessing Data for Personalized Coaching

THE KEY ADVANTAGE of wearable technology lies in its ability to provide real-time, accurate data. From heart rate monitoring to tracking steps and sleep patterns, wearables offer a wealth of information. The art of personalized coaching involves interpreting this data to tailor fitness programs that cater to individual client needs. For instance, if a client's data shows decreased activity levels or disrupted sleep patterns, a coach can adjust the training regimen accordingly.

Choosing the Right Wearable Technology

WITH A MYRIAD OF OPTIONS AVAILABLE, selecting the right wearable technology is crucial. Consider factors like accuracy, ease of use, compatibility with other platforms, and the specific metrics it tracks. Devices like Fitbit, Apple Watch, and Garmin offer varied features suitable for different coaching needs. The choice of device should align with your coaching style and the specific needs of your clientele.

Integration with Coaching Platforms

TO MAXIMIZE the benefits of wearable technology, integrate it with your coaching platform. This integration allows for seamless data transfer and analysis, providing a comprehensive view of each client's progress. It enables coaches to make data-driven decisions, adjust training plans in real time, and provide feedback based on tangible metrics.

Educating Clients on Wearable Use

A SIGNIFICANT PART of leveraging wearable technology is educating clients on its proper use and the interpretation of data. Ensure that clients understand how to wear the devices correctly and interpret the data they provide. This education empowers clients to be active participants in their fitness journey, enhancing their engagement and commitment to the program.

Data Privacy and Security

WHEN DEALING with sensitive client data, privacy and security are paramount. Ensure that the wearables and platforms you use comply with data protection regulations. Educate clients about data privacy and secure their consent for data collection and analysis. This transparency builds trust and ensures a secure coaching environment.

Analyzing Data for Enhanced Coaching

THE POWER of wearable technology lies in the insights derived from data analysis. Analyze trends over time to gain a deeper understanding of each client's progress and challenges. This analysis can reveal patterns that inform more effective training strategies, dietary recommendations, and lifestyle adjustments.

Actionable Steps for Coaches

- **Research and Select Appropriate Wearables:** Choose devices that align with your coaching style and client needs.

- **Integrate Wearables with Coaching Platforms:** Ensure seamless data flow between devices and your coaching software.
- **Educate Clients:** Teach clients how to use wearables effectively and understand the data they provide.
- **Prioritize Data Privacy:** Comply with data protection regulations and maintain client trust.
- **Analyze and Apply Data Insights:** Regularly review data to tailor training programs and provide personalized coaching.
- **Continuous Learning:** Stay updated with the latest developments in wearable technology to enhance your coaching techniques.

IN CONCLUSION, wearable technology has opened new frontiers in fitness coaching, offering unprecedented opportunities for personalized training. By effectively leveraging data from wearables, fitness professionals can enhance client engagement, track progress accurately, and deliver results more effectively. As we embrace this technological evolution, coaches who adeptly integrate and utilize these tools will lead the charge in the future of personalized fitness coaching. Remember, in the digital age of fitness, data-driven coaching is not just an option; it's a necessity for those who aspire to lead and innovate.

Part 2: Online Marketing and Client Acquisition

SEO Strategies for Fitness Coaches

"IMAGINE a world where your fitness coaching business is the first one a potential client finds online. That's the power of SEO," said a renowned digital marketing expert. This vivid illustration brings us to the heart of SEO strategies for fitness coaches, a crucial aspect for boosting online visibility and attracting more clients. In this section, we explore the nitty-gritty of implementing SEO techniques, focusing on keyword optimization and content creation to achieve higher search rankings.

Understanding the Importance of SEO

SEO, or Search Engine Optimization, is the art of making your website more visible on search engines like Google. When someone searches for fitness coaching, you want your website to be among the top results. This visibility is crucial because most people do not look beyond the first page of search results.

Keyword Optimization: The First Step to Success

KEYWORDS ARE the words or phrases that potential clients use when they search for fitness coaching services online. Your first task is to identify the right keywords that align with your coaching services. Tools like Google Keyword Planner or SEMrush can help you discover popular search terms in your niche. Once you have a list of relevant keywords, integrate them naturally into your website's content, including titles, headers, and main text.

Content Creation: Providing Value to Your Audience

CONTENT IS king in the world of SEO. Creating informative, engaging, and keyword-rich content is essential for improving your website's ranking. This can be in the form of blog posts, articles, or even videos that address common questions, offer fitness tips, or share success stories. Regularly updating your website with fresh content not only attracts search engines but also keeps visitors coming back.

On-Page SEO: Optimizing Your Website

ON-PAGE SEO INVOLVES OPTIMIZING the elements of your website for search engines. This includes incorporating keywords into your meta descriptions, alt tags for images, and creating SEO-friendly URLs. It also means ensuring your website is mobile-friendly, as more and more users are accessing the internet via smartphones.

Off-Page SEO: Building Your Website's Reputation

OFF-PAGE SEO REFERS to actions taken outside of your own website to impact your rankings within search engine results pages. This primarily involves building backlinks - links from other reputable websites to yours. Guest blogging on popular fitness sites, participating in online fitness forums, and being active on social media can help build these valuable links.

Measuring SEO Success

TRACK your SEO efforts to see what's working. Google Analytics is an invaluable tool for monitoring your website's traffic, understanding your audience's behavior, and seeing which keywords are driving the most visitors.

Actionable Steps for Fitness Coaches

- **Research and Use Relevant Keywords:** Identify keywords related to your fitness niche and integrate them into your website content.
- **Create Quality Content Regularly:** Publish informative and engaging articles, blog posts, or videos that provide value to your audience.
- **Optimize Your Website:** Ensure your website is mobile-friendly, fast-loading, and uses SEO-friendly URLs.
- **Build Backlinks:** Guest post on reputable fitness websites and participate in online communities to build backlinks.
- **Monitor Your Progress:** Use tools like Google Analytics to track your website's performance and adjust your strategies accordingly.

MASTERING SEO IS a powerful way for fitness coaches to enhance their online visibility and attract more clients. By carefully selecting keywords, creating valuable content, and optimizing your website, you can climb the search engine rankings and make your fitness coaching business more accessible to potential clients. Remember, SEO is not a one-time task but a continuous process that requires regular attention and adjustment. Embrace these strategies, and watch your online presence grow, bringing more opportunities for success in the digital world of fitness coaching.

Social Media Marketing

"DID you know that over 70% of consumers expect a brand to have a social media presence?" This startling fact underscores the importance of social media marketing for fitness coaches. In a world where digital interaction is key, crafting an effective social media strategy for client acquisition is not just beneficial, it's essential. This section will delve into creating a robust social media presence, focusing on engaging with your audience and utilizing various platforms effectively.

Crafting Your Social Media Persona

THE FIRST STEP is to define your brand's persona on social media. This persona should align with your coaching style and values. Are you the motivational coach who inspires with high-energy posts? Or are you more about mindfulness and wellness? Your social media should reflect the unique aspects of your fitness coaching.

Choosing the Right Platforms

NOT ALL SOCIAL media platforms are created equal, especially when it comes to fitness coaching. Instagram and YouTube are great for visual content like workout videos and transformation photos, while Twitter is ideal for sharing quick fitness tips. Facebook, with its vast user base, is excellent for building a community and engaging in longer-form discussions.

Content Creation: The Heart of Engagement

CONTENT IS the fuel for your social media strategy. Your posts should be a mix of educational content, motivational stories, client testimonials, and behind-the-scenes glimpses into your coaching life. Remember, consistency is key. Regular posting keeps your audience engaged and helps build a loyal following.

Engaging with Your Audience

ENGAGEMENT IS NOT JUST about posting content; it's about interacting with your audience. Respond to comments, participate in discussions, and encourage your followers to share their fitness journeys. These interactions build a community around your brand, which is invaluable for client acquisition.

Utilizing Stories and Live Sessions

STORIES and live sessions on platforms like Instagram and Facebook are powerful tools. They offer a real-time, interactive way to connect with your audience. Use these features for live Q&A sessions, workout demonstrations, or sharing motivational stories.

Hashtags and Collaborations

HASHTAGS CAN DRASTICALLY INCREASE the visibility of your posts. Use relevant hashtags related to fitness, wellness, and coaching. Collaborating with other fitness professionals or brands on social media can also broaden your reach and bring in new followers.

Analyzing Your Social Media Performance

TO UNDERSTAND WHAT WORKS BEST, regularly analyze your social media performance. Tools like Google Analytics and social media platform insights can provide data on post engagement, follower growth, and the best times to post.

Actionable Steps for Fitness Coaches

- **Define Your Social Media Persona:** Align your online presence with your coaching style and values.
- **Choose the Right Platforms:** Focus on platforms that best suit your content and audience.
- **Create Engaging Content:** Mix educational, motivational, and personal content. Post consistently.

- **Interact with Your Audience:** Engage in conversations, respond to comments, and build a community.
- **Utilize Stories and Live Features:** Connect with your audience in real-time for greater engagement.
- **Leverage Hashtags and Collaborations:** Increase your visibility through strategic hashtag use and partnerships.
- **Analyze Performance:** Regularly review your social media analytics to refine your strategy.

IN CONCLUSION, social media marketing is a dynamic and powerful tool for fitness coaches looking to acquire new clients and build their brand. By carefully crafting your social media strategy, engaging with your audience, and regularly evaluating your performance, you can maximize the benefits of these platforms. Embrace the digital world, and watch as your fitness coaching business reaches new heights in the online space. Remember, your social media presence is an extension of your coaching philosophy – make it count.

Email Marketing and Newsletters

"AN EMAIL CAN BRIDGE the gap between relevance and obscurity in the blink of an eye," a renowned marketing expert once said. This statement rings especially true for fitness coaches navigating the digital landscape. Email marketing and newsletters are powerful tools that, when wielded correctly, can significantly boost a fitness coach's ability to reach and retain clients. In this part of the chapter, we will explore how to effectively use email marketing and develop newsletters that not only provide value but also drive engagement.

Creating a Strong Email Marketing Foundation

BEFORE DIVING into the intricacies of newsletters, it's essential to establish a robust email marketing strategy. This involves building a healthy email list. Begin by encouraging your website visitors and social media followers to subscribe. Offer them compelling reasons, such as exclusive content or early access to programs and discounts.

Understanding Your Audience

KNOW YOUR AUDIENCE. Tailor your emails to meet their interests, goals, and challenges. Segmentation is key; not all subscribers are at the same fitness level or interested in the same type of content. Customize your emails to address these varied interests.

Crafting Engaging Newsletters

YOUR NEWSLETTER IS MORE than just a promotional tool; it's a reflection of your expertise and passion for fitness. Include a mix of content: workout tips, nutritional advice, success stories, and personal insights into your coaching journey. Remember, quality trumps quantity.

Subject Lines That Stand Out

THE SUBJECT LINE is your first impression. Make it count. Use compelling, clear, and concise language that prompts your subscribers to open the email. Avoid clickbait; be honest about the content of your email.

Personalization and Authenticity

ADDRESS YOUR SUBSCRIBERS by name to create a personal touch. Share your experiences and stories, making your emails feel like a conversation rather than a sales pitch. Authenticity builds trust and fosters a stronger connection with your audience.

. . .

Mobile Optimization

WITH MOST EMAILS being opened on mobile devices, ensure your newsletters are mobile-friendly. Use responsive design templates that adapt to different screen sizes for a seamless reading experience.

Consistency and Timing

CONSISTENCY IS CRUCIAL. Decide on a frequency for your newsletters and stick to it. Test different days and times for sending your emails to see when you get the best engagement.

Call to Action

EVERY EMAIL SHOULD HAVE a clear call to action (CTA). Whether it's to book a session, follow you on social media, or read your latest blog post, your CTA should be clear and direct.

Measuring Success

TRACK your email performance through metrics like open rates, click-through rates, and conversion rates. These insights will help you refine your strategy and content over time.

Actionable Steps for Fitness Coaches

- **Build a Quality Email List:** Encourage sign-ups through your website and social media.
- **Segment Your Audience:** Tailor your content to different groups within your audience.

- **Create Valuable Content:** Mix educational, motivational, and personal content in your newsletters.
- **Craft Compelling Subject Lines:** Make them clear, engaging, and reflective of the email's content.
- **Personalize Your Emails:** Use names and share personal stories for a more authentic connection.
- **Optimize for Mobile:** Ensure your emails are readable on all devices.
- **Maintain Consistency:** Stick to a regular schedule for sending out your newsletters.
- **Include Clear CTAs:** Direct your readers to take the desired action.
- **Analyze and Adapt:** Regularly check your email metrics and adjust your strategy accordingly.

IN SUMMARY, email marketing and newsletters are about building and nurturing relationships with your clients and prospects. It's a blend of art and science, requiring a keen understanding of your audience's needs and consistent, valuable engagement. By mastering these aspects, you can turn your email marketing into a pivotal component of your fitness coaching business, ensuring both reach and retention of clients. Remember, in the world of email marketing, it's not just about selling; it's about connecting and providing undeniable value.

Online Advertising and Promotions

"IN THE REALM of online advertising, it's not about the big budget; it's about the big idea." This quote encapsulates the essence of successful online campaigns for fitness coaches. The art of crafting compelling online advertising and promotions lies in understanding the intersection of creativity, strategy, and technology. This section will explore the various facets of online advertising and how fitness coaches can create campaigns that resonate with their target audience.

. . .

Understanding Online Advertising Providers

Navigating the world of online advertising begins with understanding the platforms available. Each platform, whether it's Google Ads, Facebook, Instagram, or others, has its unique features and audience demographics. Fitness coaches must choose platforms that align with where their target audience spends most of their time online.

Crafting Your Campaign

The heart of a successful campaign is a compelling message. Start by defining the unique selling proposition (USP) of your fitness services. What makes your approach special? How does it transform the lives of your clients? Your campaign should communicate this clearly and persuasively.

Target Audience Identification

Identifying and understanding your target audience is crucial. Who are they? What are their fitness goals? What challenges do they face? A deep understanding of your audience will guide the tone, content, and visual elements of your campaign.

Creating Engaging Content

Content is king in online advertising. Use high-quality images, engaging videos, and persuasive copy to capture attention. Remember, your content should not only attract but also add value to your audience. Educational and inspirational content often performs well in the fitness industry.

Optimizing for Keywords

SEO PLAYS a significant role in online advertising. Research and use keywords that your target audience is likely to search for. This enhances the visibility of your ads and drives more relevant traffic to your website or landing page.

A/B Testing

EXPERIMENTATION IS key to refining your campaigns. Use A/B testing to compare different versions of your ads. This helps identify what resonates best with your audience, whether it's a particular image, headline, or call to action.

Monitoring and Adjusting Campaigns

THE DIGITAL LANDSCAPE IS DYNAMIC. Regularly monitor your campaigns and be ready to adjust based on performance data. Analyze metrics like click-through rates, conversion rates, and return on investment to gauge the effectiveness of your campaigns.

Actionable Steps for Fitness Coaches

CHOOSE THE RIGHT PLATFORM: Select advertising platforms that align with your target audience.

- **Define Your USP:** Clearly articulate what sets your fitness services apart.
- **Know Your Audience:** Tailor your campaign to the specific needs and preferences of your target market.
- **Create Quality Content:** Use engaging visuals and compelling copy.
- **Optimize for Keywords:** Incorporate relevant keywords for better visibility.
- **Experiment with A/B Testing:** Test different elements of your ads to see what works best.

- **Monitor and Adapt:** Regularly review your campaign's performance and make necessary adjustments.

ONLINE ADVERTISING and promotions offer an expansive canvas for fitness coaches to showcase their expertise and connect with potential clients. It's about combining creativity with strategy and technology. By understanding your audience, crafting compelling campaigns, and continuously refining your approach, you can leverage online advertising to significantly boost your online visibility and client acquisition. Remember, in the digital world, the most resonant message is one that speaks directly to the needs and aspirations of your audience.

Part 3: Virtual Coaching and Client Management

Transitioning to Virtual Coaching

IMAGINE A SEASONED FITNESS COACH, known for their dynamic in-person sessions, suddenly faced with the challenge of transitioning to virtual coaching. This shift, though daunting, opened new avenues for innovation and adaptation. This section of the chapter delves into the intricacies of adapting one's coaching style for effective virtual sessions and addresses the common challenges faced in the realm of virtual coaching and training.

Adapting Coaching Style for Virtual Sessions

THE TRANSITION to virtual coaching requires a fundamental shift in approach. The first step is understanding the limitations and advantages of the virtual format. While the physical presence is lost, the opportunity to use technology to monitor progress and maintain engagement is gained. Coaches need to become adept at using digital tools to track workouts, monitor clients' form, and provide feedback.

Creating Engaging Virtual Sessions

ENGAGEMENT IS key in virtual sessions. Without the energy of a physical gym environment, it's crucial to keep clients motivated and focused. This can be achieved through interactive workouts, using visuals and music to create an engaging atmosphere. Personalizing sessions to each client's preferences and fitness goals can also significantly boost engagement.

Communication is Key

CLEAR AND EFFECTIVE communication becomes even more critical in a virtual setting. Coaches must ensure instructions are concise and easy to understand. Regular check-ins and feedback sessions can help maintain a personal connection and address any concerns or adjustments needed in the training plan.

Overcoming Technical Challenges

VIRTUAL COACHING IS HEAVILY reliant on technology, which can sometimes be a barrier. Coaches should be prepared to troubleshoot common technical issues like connectivity problems or software glitches. It's also important to guide clients through setting up their space and equipment for optimal training sessions.

Maintaining Personal Connection

BUILDING AND MAINTAINING a personal connection with clients is challenging but not impossible in a virtual setting. Coaches can use video calls to maintain face-to-face interactions and take extra time to discuss clients' progress and challenges, making the sessions more than just about workouts.

Actionable Steps for Virtual Coaching

- **Embrace Technology:** Familiarize yourself with various online platforms and digital tools that can enhance virtual coaching.
- **Interactive Sessions:** Use interactive elements to keep clients engaged during workouts.
- **Clear Communication:** Develop the ability to give clear, concise instructions and feedback.
- **Technical Preparedness:** Be ready to handle technical issues and guide clients through them.
- **Personalize Training:** Tailor sessions to each client's needs, preferences, and goals.

- **Regular Check-ins:** Have frequent discussions with clients about their progress and any challenges they're facing.

TRANSITIONING to virtual coaching requires flexibility, creativity, and a willingness to embrace new methods. By adapting your coaching style, embracing technology, and maintaining a personal connection with clients, you can overcome the challenges and continue to provide effective training and support in a virtual format. The key is to view these challenges not as obstacles but as opportunities to grow and innovate in your coaching practice.

Online Coaching Platforms

"IN THE REALM OF FITNESS, the true art lies not just in training the body, but in leveraging the right tools to amplify your reach and impact." This adage rings especially true in today's digital age, where online coaching platforms have revolutionized the way fitness professionals connect with clients. In this section, we will explore the intricacies of online coaching platforms for virtual training and how they can be maximized for both client benefit and business growth.

LET'S consider the story of Laura, a personal trainer who transitioned from traditional gym-based training to online coaching. Initially skeptical about the effectiveness of virtual training, Laura was amazed at the increased engagement and satisfaction levels among her clients, as well as the growth in her business. Her journey exemplifies the transformative power of online platforms in the fitness industry.

Understanding Online Coaching Platforms

ONLINE COACHING PLATFORMS are more than just video calling tools. They are comprehensive systems that enable fitness professionals to manage every aspect of their training programs. These platforms often include features like workout plan creation, progress tracking, client communication channels, and even payment processing. The key is to choose a platform that aligns with your coaching style and business needs.

Selecting the Right Platform

THE FIRST STEP is to identify what you need from an online coaching platform. Consider factors like ease of use, customization options, integration with other tools, and cost. Platforms like Trainerize, TrueCoach, or My PT Hub offer various features tailored to different coaching styles. It's crucial to select a platform that not only suits your style but also provides an excellent user experience for your clients.

Maximizing Client Engagement

ENGAGEMENT IS the cornerstone of successful online coaching. Utilize the interactive features of your chosen platform to keep your clients motivated. This can include setting up regular check-ins, using progress trackers, and offering personalized feedback. Interactive elements like gamification, where clients earn badges or rewards for reaching milestones, can significantly boost motivation and adherence to the program.

Program Management and Customization

A MAJOR ADVANTAGE of online platforms is the ability to manage and customize training programs efficiently. Use the platform to create tailored workout plans, track client progress, and adjust programs based on feedback. This level of customization helps in addressing the unique goals and challenges of each client, leading to better results and higher client satisfaction.

. . .

Building Your Online Presence

YOUR ONLINE PRESENCE is crucial in attracting and retaining clients. Use your platform to showcase your expertise, share client success stories, and provide valuable fitness content. Engage with your clients through the platform's communication channels, creating a community that supports and motivates each other.

Marketing Your Online Coaching Services

EFFECTIVE MARKETING IS key to growing your online coaching business. Utilize social media, email marketing, and your personal network to promote your services. Offer free trials or introductory sessions to attract potential clients. Encourage satisfied clients to share their experiences and refer others to your services.

Analyzing and Adapting

REGULARLY ANALYZE the performance of your online coaching services. Gather feedback from clients, monitor engagement metrics, and assess the financial aspects of your business. Use this data to continually refine your approach and adapt to changing client needs and market trends.

ONLINE COACHING PLATFORMS offer a dynamic and effective way to train clients virtually. By carefully selecting the right platform, maximizing client engagement, managing programs efficiently, and continually adapting to feedback, fitness professionals can not only enhance their clients' experience but also grow their businesses substantially. The digital age has opened up new horizons in fitness coaching, and those who embrace these opportunities are poised for success. Remember, the goal is not just to train but to transform lives, and online coaching platforms are powerful tools in achieving this mission.

Application of Techniques:

Leveraging Fitness and Health Apps

- Scenario: A coach uses an app for personalized workout plans. Example: Sarah incorporates 'MyFitnessPal' for nutrition tracking and 'Strava' for workout logging, enabling real-time monitoring and feedback for clients.
- Process: Select apps complementing your coaching style, test them, educate clients on usage, and routinely gather feedback for adjustments.

Website Development and Management

- Scenario: Revamping a website to enhance user engagement. Example: Emily transforms her basic website into an interactive hub with a blog, online booking, and client testimonials.
- Process: Focus on user-friendly design, responsive layouts, engaging content, strong CTAs, SEO optimization, social media integration, and online scheduling.

Using Wearable Technology

- Scenario: Integrating wearables for data-driven coaching. Example: A coach uses Fitbit data to customize workout plans based on clients' sleep patterns and activity levels.
- Process: Select wearables aligning with coaching needs, educate clients on usage, integrate data with

coaching platforms, and prioritize data privacy and security.

SEO Strategies for Fitness Coaches

- Scenario: Optimizing a fitness blog to attract more clients. Example: Using keywords like "home workouts" and "nutrition tips" in blog posts to improve search rankings.
- Process: Identify relevant keywords, create quality content, optimize website elements, build backlinks, and regularly monitor SEO performance.

Social Media Marketing

- Scenario: Boosting client engagement through Instagram. Example: Posting daily workout tips, client transformation stories, and engaging through live Q&A sessions.
- Process: Define social media persona, choose suitable platforms, create varied content, interact with followers, utilize stories and lives, and analyze performance.

Email Marketing and Newsletters:

- Scenario: Launching a newsletter to keep clients informed and engaged. Example: Sending bi-weekly emails with fitness tips, success stories, and personal coaching insights.
- Process: Build an email list, segment audience, craft engaging newsletters, use compelling subject lines,

personalize content, optimize for mobile, and include clear CTAs.

Online Advertising and Promotions:

- Scenario: Running a Facebook ad campaign for a new fitness program. Example: Targeting ads to fitness enthusiasts in a specific age group and geographical area.
- Process: Understand online advertising platforms, craft compelling campaigns, identify target audience, create engaging content, optimize for keywords, A/B test ads, and adjust based on performance.

Transitioning to Virtual Coaching:

- Scenario: Shifting from in-person to online coaching. Example: Using Zoom for live sessions and Slack for client communication and support.
- Process: Adapt coaching style for virtual delivery, create engaging sessions, maintain clear communication, overcome technical challenges, and maintain a personal connection with clients.

Online Coaching Platforms:

- Scenario: Managing client programs through an online platform. Example: Laura uses Trainerize to track client workouts, provide feedback, and manage schedules.
- Process: Select a platform that matches your coaching style, maximize client engagement, manage programs

effectively, build an online presence, market services, and continually adapt based on feedback.

Action Item Checklist:

IDENTIFY Suitable Fitness and Health Apps:

- Research various fitness apps.
- Test each app for compatibility with your coaching style.
- Educate clients on how to use these apps effectively.

DEVELOP AND MANAGE YOUR WEBSITE:

- Choose a user-friendly website builder.
- Create engaging, SEO-optimized content.
- Regularly update your site with fresh content and features.

INTEGRATE WEARABLE TECHNOLOGY:

- Select wearable devices that suit your training style.
- Teach clients how to use these devices and interpret data.
- Use data to tailor fitness programs and track progress.

IMPLEMENT SEO STRATEGIES:

- Conduct keyword research relevant to your fitness niche.
- Create and regularly update SEO-rich content on your site.
- Monitor your website's SEO performance and make necessary adjustments.

CRAFT A SOCIAL MEDIA MARKETING PLAN:

- Define your brand's social media persona.
- Create a content calendar for regular posting.
- Engage with followers through comments, messages, and live sessions.

LAUNCH AN EMAIL MARKETING CAMPAIGN:

- Build an email list through your website and social media.
- Segment your audience based on their interests and fitness levels.
- Design and send out regular, personalized newsletters.

CREATE ONLINE ADVERTISING CAMPAIGNS:

- Select the appropriate advertising platforms.
- Develop engaging ad content with a clear message.
- Monitor ad performance and tweak for better results.

TRANSITION TO EFFECTIVE VIRTUAL COACHING:

- Familiarize yourself with various online coaching tools and platforms.
- Conduct trial sessions to iron out any technical kinks.
- Maintain regular communication with clients for feedback and progress tracking.

UTILIZE ONLINE COACHING PLATFORMS:

- Choose a platform that offers comprehensive features for virtual coaching.
- Utilize the platform's tools for client management and engagement.
- Continuously seek client feedback to improve the online coaching experience.

Resource List:

TOOLS:

- **Fitness Apps:** MyFitnessPal, Strava, Trainerize.
- **Website Builders:** WordPress, Wix, Squarespace.
- **Wearable Devices:** Fitbit, Apple Watch, Garmin.
- **SEO Tools:** Google Keyword Planner, SEMrush.
- **Social Media Platforms:** Instagram, Facebook, Twitter.
- **Email Marketing Services:** Mailchimp, Constant Contact.
- **Online Advertising Platforms:** Google Ads, Facebook Ads.
- **Virtual Coaching Tools:** Zoom, Slack.

BOOKS AND READING MATERIAL:

- **"Digital Marketing for Dummies"** - A comprehensive guide to digital marketing strategies.
- **"The Personal Trainer's Handbook"** - Provides insights into adapting fitness coaching for the digital age.

ADDITIONAL RESOURCES:

- **Online Courses:** Udemy courses on digital marketing, SEO, and social media strategies.
- **Websites:** HubSpot Blog for marketing tips, Fitness Business Association for industry trends.
- **Forums:** Bodybuilding.com forums, Reddit's r/fitness for community engagement.

conclusion

. . .

AS WE DRAW the curtains on this enlightening journey through "How to Start a Fitness Coaching and Training Business: A Step-by-Step Guide to Profitable Fitness Programs and Personal Trainer Entrepreneurship," it's clear that the path to success in this vibrant industry is as rewarding as it is challenging. This book has not only served as a guide but also as a companion, illuminating the path for aspiring fitness entrepreneurs to carve their niche in the ever-evolving landscape of fitness coaching.

REFLECTING ON THE JOURNEY, we began by laying the foundation for your fitness coaching business. Understanding the fitness industry landscape and identifying your niche were our starting points, essential for anyone looking to make a mark in this dynamic field. We delved into assessing the market, analyzing fitness industry trends, understanding client demographics, and conducting a thorough competitor analysis. These initial steps were crucial in crafting a comprehensive business plan, setting clear and achievable goals for your business growth.

. . .

ESTABLISHING your brand was our next milestone. We explored creating a unique brand identity, developing a fitness philosophy, and building an online presence. The significance of networking and forming strategic partnerships was emphasized, highlighting the importance of community and collaboration in the fitness industry.

NAVIGATING legal and financial considerations formed a critical part of our journey. We covered the essentials of understanding legal requirements, setting up financial systems, insurance, liability, and pricing your services. This knowledge is vital in establishing a business that is not only fit in terms of health but also robust in its financial and legal standing.

DESIGNING profitable fitness programs was a chapter that resonated with the core of fitness coaching. We discussed understanding client needs, incorporating diverse training modalities, creating scalable programs, and staying ahead with innovative program designs. Marketing these programs effectively, leveraging client testimonials, mastering social media, and building a referral network were key strategies we explored for attracting and retaining clients.

IN MASTERING the art of personal trainer entrepreneurship, we emphasized developing an entrepreneurial mindset, acquiring essential business skills, and continuous learning and development. Financial management, budgeting, diversification of revenue streams, and investment in growth and expansion were also critical areas we touched upon.

NAVIGATING the digital landscape for fitness coaching brought us to the forefront of technological advancements in the fitness industry. We covered leveraging fitness and health apps, website development and management, and the use of wearable technology. Online marketing and client acquisition strategies, such as

SEO, social media marketing, email marketing, and online advertising, were explored in depth.

As we close this chapter, remember that your journey as a fitness coach is unique and ever-evolving. The strategies, tips, and insights shared in this book are your tools – use them to build a business that not only reflects your passion and expertise but also stands tall in the competitive fitness industry. Embrace the challenges, celebrate the victories, and continue to grow and adapt. Your journey in the world of fitness coaching and training is just beginning, and the possibilities are limitless.

Remember, the fitness industry is not just about physical strength; it's about resilience, adaptability, and the relentless pursuit of excellence. As you step out to make your mark, carry with you the lessons, insights, and strategies from this book. Let them guide you, inspire you, and push you towards achieving your dreams. Your journey in the fitness industry is a testament to your passion, dedication, and entrepreneurial spirit – qualities that define a successful fitness coach and entrepreneur.